SCHOLASTIC News Leveled Informational Texts

New York • Toronto • London • Auckland • Sydney
Mexico City • New Delhi • Hong Kong • Buenos Aires

Photos ©: cover left: Barcroft/Getty Images; cover center: iLite Photography; cover right: Bettman/Getty Images; cover bottom: Jim Abernethy/ Getty Images; back cover bottom left: iLite Photography; back cover bottom right: Jim Abernethy/Getty Images; 3 top left: fitopardo.com/Getty Images; 3 bottom left: Eric Isselee/Shutterstock; 3 bottom right and throughout: Koji Sasahara/AP Images; 6 top right and throughout: Pete Oxford/ Minden Pictures/GettyImages; 6 bottom left and throughout: Jeff Vanuga/Getty Images; 6 bottom right and throughout: Cordier Sylvain/hemis.fr/ GettyImages; 7 bottom right map: negoworks/iStockphoto; 12 and throughout: Koji Sasahara/AP Images; 18 and throughout: mlharing/iStockphoto; 19 and throughout: Anneka/Shutterstock; 25 and throughout: Sergey Nivens/Shutterstock; 31 and throughout: Benjamin Albiach Galan/Shutterstock; 32 and throughout: 11qq22/Shutterstock; 39 and throughout: Barcroft/Getty Images; 41 and throughout: Courtesy of Noah's Ark Sanctuary; 48 and throughout: Underwood Archives/Getty Images; 50 and throughout: Joseph Sohm/Shutterstock; 57 and throughout: Kerry Hargrove/Shutterstock; 59 top and throughout: Yasmins world/Shutterstock; 59 bottom and throughout: John E Marriott/Getty Images; 67 and throughout: iLite Photography; 69 and throughout: Source: Loon. Maps by Jim McMahon, Scholastic Inc.

Editor: Maria L. Chang
Cover design by Michelle H. Kim
Interior design by Kay Petronio

Scholastic Inc., 557 Broadway, New York, NY 10012
ISBN: 978-1-338-28473-7
Copyright © 2019 by Scholastic Inc.
All rights reserved.
Printed in the U.S.A.
First printing, January 2019.

1 2 3 4 5 6 7 8 9 10   40   25 24 23 22 21 20 19

Table of Contents

Introduction

Finding quality informational texts at the appropriate level can be quite challenging. That's why we created this collection of compelling articles, which were originally printed in our award-winning classroom magazine *Scholastic News*. The passages have been carefully selected to engage students' interest and have been leveled to meet the needs of all readers. Each article comes in three Lexile levels. But because all versions of an article look alike, students need not know they're getting different levels. To identify the reading levels, simply look at the shape around the page numbers.

△ – **below level (500L–600L)**

○ – **on level (600L–700L)**

☐ – **above level (700L–800L)**

Each article comes with a variety of comprehension questions, including multiple choice, short response, and essay. These questions challenge students to identify the main idea and supporting details; make inferences; determine cause and effect; identify author's purpose and point of view; interpret maps, charts, and diagrams; build vocabulary; summarize; and more. In fact, you can use this book to help students get ready for standardized tests.

One way to build students' comprehension is to encourage them to mark up the text as they read—circling, underlining, or highlighting main ideas, supporting details, and key vocabulary words. This simple action helps them process what they're reading, making it easier to focus on important ideas and make connections. For more test-taking tips, photocopy and distribute the helpful hints below for students.

TEST-TAKING TIPS FOR STUDENTS:

- Make sure you understand each question fully before you answer it. Underline key words. Restate the question in your own words.

- Always refer to the text to find answers. It's a good idea to go back and reread parts of the text to answer a question.

- When you finish, check all your answers. You may find a mistake that you can correct.

- Most important, relax! Some people get nervous before a test. That's normal. Just do your best.

They're Back

1   The past 200 years have been hard for many animals around the world. Their homes in the wild have been destroyed. People cut them down to make room for houses, farms, and roads. Other types of animals have been overhunted.

2   More than 3,000 types of animals are close to dying out. **Conservation groups** have been working hard to save those animals. Now some troubled animals are making comebacks.

Greater One-Horned Rhinoceros

3   Greater one-horned rhinoceroses live in South Asia. There used to be thousands of them. But by the early 1900s, fewer than 200 rhinos were left in the wild. Many were hunted for their horns. The government made it against the law to hunt rhinos. Now about 2,600 rhinos live in the wild.

Lear's Macaw

4   The Lear's macaw is a blue parrot. It's found only in Brazil. This bird was discovered in 1978. But by the late 1980s, only 70 were left. The trees in which they lived were being cut down.

5   Conservation groups bought 4,000 acres of the birds' rainforest home. This helped. By 2009, their numbers had grown to 950.

Black-Footed Ferrets

6   Thousands of black-footed ferrets used to live across the central United States and Canada. But some people thought they were pests and killed them. By the mid-1970s, these ferrets seemed to have disappeared.

7   But in 1981, a group of 18 ferrets was found in Wyoming. They were taken to a special center. Their numbers grew. Today, about 500 ferrets live in the wild.

Ranges of Comeback Species

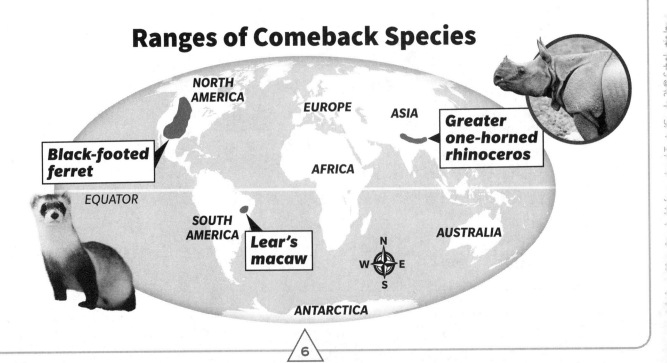

Name: _____

Directions: Read the article "They're Back." Then answer the questions below.

1. Which sentence best describes the animals featured in the article?

    A. Their numbers are growing again.

    B. They are all being hunted.

    C. They all live in the rainforest.

    D. There are too many of them.

2. Which sentence from the article supports your answer in question 1?

    A. The past 200 years have been hard for many animals around the world. *(paragraph 1)*

    B. More than 3,000 types of animals are close to dying out. *(paragraph 2)*

    C. Now some troubled animals are making comebacks. *(paragraph 2)*

    D. But by the early 1900s, fewer than 200 rhinos were left in the wild. *(paragraph 3)*

3. Read this sentence from paragraph 2.

    Conservation groups have been working hard to save those animals.

  What does the term *conservation groups* mean as used in the article?

    A. People who protect valuable things, such as wildlife and the environment

    B. People who treat sick or injured animals

    C. People who talk to one another

    D. People who hunt animals for food or sport

4. How does the information on the map support the article?

    A. It shows the location of conservation groups.

    B. It shows the location of the animals described in the article.

    C. It shows the continents of the world and the equator.

    D. It shows the places where animals are most endangered.

5. The article says that conservation groups bought land in Brazil to protect a type of macaw. How would that help the macaws make a comeback? Use details from the article to support your answer.

Brazil

_____

_____

_____

_____

They're Back

1   For many animals around the world, the past 200 years have been rough. Their homes in the wild have been destroyed by people to make room for houses, farms, and roads. Other types of animals have been overhunted.

2   More than 3,000 types of animals are now endangered, or close to dying out. **Conservation groups** have been working hard to save those animals. That work is paying off. Now some troubled animals are making comebacks.

Greater One-Horned Rhinoceros

3   Greater one-horned rhinoceroses live in the forests of South Asia. There used to be thousands of them. But by the early 1900s, fewer than 200 rhinos were left in the wild. Many were hunted for their horns.

4   Conservation groups helped make hunting rhinos against the law. Now about 2,600 rhinos live in the wild.

Lear's Macaw

5   The Lear's macaw is a blue parrot that's found only in Brazil. This bird was discovered in 1978. But by the late 1980s, only 70 were left. The trees in which they lived were being cut down. Conservation groups bought 4,000 acres of the birds' rainforest home. This helped the macaws. By 2009, the parrots' numbers had grown to more than 950.

Black-Footed Ferret

6   Thousands of black-footed ferrets once lived across the central United States and Canada. But some people thought they were pests and killed them. By the mid-1970s, these ferrets seemed to have disappeared.

7   But in 1981, a group of 18 ferrets was found in Wyoming. They were taken to a special center. Their numbers grew. Today, about 500 ferrets live in the wild.

Ranges of Comeback Species

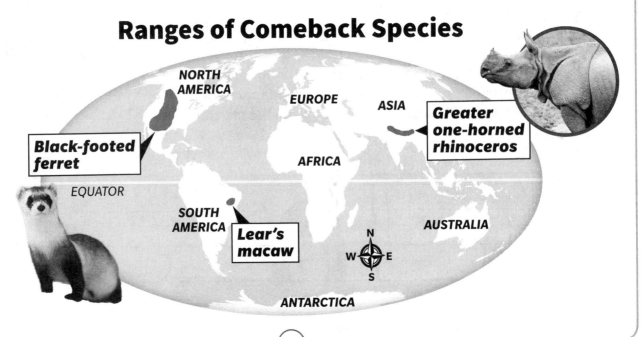

NORTH AMERICA

EUROPE

ASIA

Greater one-horned rhinoceros

Black-footed ferret

AFRICA

EQUATOR

SOUTH AMERICA

Lear's macaw

AUSTRALIA

N
W E
S

ANTARCTICA

Name: _____

Directions: Read the article "They're Back." Then answer the questions below.

1. Which sentence best describes the animals featured in the article?

    A. They all live in the rainforest.

    B. They are all being hunted.

    c. There are too many of them.

    D. Their numbers are growing again.

2. Which sentence from the article supports your answer in question 1?

    A. For many animals around the world, the past 200 years have been rough. *(paragraph 1)*

    B. Now some troubled animals are making comebacks. *(paragraph 2)*

    c. More than 3,000 types of animals are now endangered, or close to dying out. *(paragraph 2)*

    D. But by the early 1900s, fewer than 200 rhinos were left in the wild. *(paragraph 3)*

3. Read this sentence from paragraph 2.

    Conservation groups have been working hard to save those animals.

    What does the term *conservation groups* mean as used in the article?

    A. People who talk to one another

    B. People who treat sick or injured animals

    c. People who protect valuable things, such as wildlife and the environment

    D. People who hunt animals for food or sport

4. How does the information on the map support the article?

    A. It shows the location of the animals described in the article.

    B. It shows the location of conservation groups.

    c. It shows the places where animals are most endangered.

    D. It shows the continents of the world and the equator.

5. The article says that conservation groups bought land in Brazil to protect a type of macaw. How would that help the macaws make a comeback? Use details from the article to support your answer.

Brazil

_____

_____

_____

_____

They're Back

1   For many animals around the world, the past 200 years have been rough. Their homes in the wild have been wiped out by people to make room for houses, farms, and roads. Other types of animals have been overhunted.

2   More than 3,000 types of animals are now endangered, or close to dying out. Conservation groups have been working hard to save those animals from **extinction**. That work is paying off. Now some troubled species are making comebacks.

Greater One-Horned Rhinoceros

3   Greater one-horned rhinoceroses live in the forests of South Asia. They once numbered in the thousands. But by the early 1900s, fewer than 200 of the rhinos were left in the wild. Many had been hunted for their horns.

4   Several years ago, conservation groups took action. They helped make hunting rhinos against the law. Now about 2,600 of the animals roam the wild.

Lear's Macaw

5   The Lear's macaw is a blue parrot that's found only in Brazil. This bird was discovered in 1978. But by the late 1980s, only 70 were known to exist. The trees in which they lived were being cut down. To help the macaws survive, conservation groups bought 4,000 acres of the birds' rainforest habitat. By 2009, the parrots' numbers had soared past 950.

Black-Footed Ferret

6   Thousands of black-footed ferrets once lived across the central United States and Canada. But they were often thought of as pests—and killed. By the mid-1970s, these ferrets were thought to be extinct.

7   Surprisingly, a group of 18 ferrets was found in Wyoming in 1981. They were taken to a special center. As their numbers grew, the ferrets were released back into the wild. Today, about 500 live in the wild.

Ranges of Comeback Species

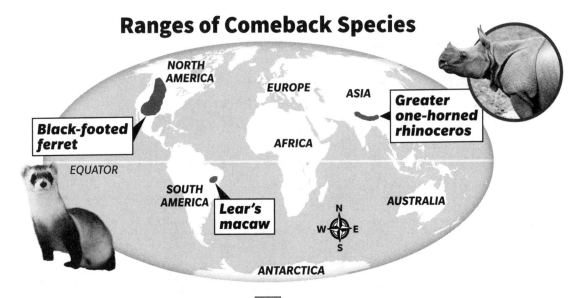

NORTH AMERICA
EUROPE
ASIA
Black-footed ferret
Greater one-horned rhinoceros
AFRICA
EQUATOR
SOUTH AMERICA
Lear's macaw
AUSTRALIA
N W E S
ANTARCTICA

Name: _____

Directions: Read the article "They're Back." Then answer the questions below.

1. Which sentence best describes the animals featured in the article?

    A. They are all being hunted.

    B. Their numbers are growing again.

    C. There are too many of them.

    D. They all live in the rainforest.

2. Which sentence from the article supports your answer in question 1?

    A. Now some troubled species are making comebacks. *(paragraph 2)*

    B. But by the early 1900s, fewer than 200 of the rhinos were left in the wild. *(paragraph 3)*

    C. More than 3,000 types of animals are now endangered, or close to dying out. *(paragraph 2)*

    D. For many animals around the world, the past 200 years have been rough. *(paragraph 1)*

3. Read this sentence from paragraph 2.

    Conservation groups have been working hard to save those animals from **extinction**.

    What does the word *extinction* mean as used in the passage?

    A. Dying out completely

    B. Surviving

    C. Having to go live somewhere else

    D. Growing in number

4. How does the information on the map support the article?

    A. It shows the location of conservation groups.

    B. It shows the location of the animals described in the article.

    C. It shows the continents of the world and the equator.

    D. It shows the places where animals are most endangered.

5. The article says that conservation groups bought land in Brazil to protect a type of macaw. How would that help the macaws make a comeback? Use details from the article to support your answer.

Brazil

_____

_____

_____

Teaching Machines

1   Is there someone in your classroom who helps your teacher? In South Korea and Japan, some schools have robots to do just that.

Language Teachers

2   In South Korea, learning English is important. But there are not enough English teachers. That's why some schools use robots. These robots help teach students how to speak English. They also read stories to the students in English. The government plans to add many more robots to their schools.

Say Hi to Saya

3   Most robots look like machines. Not Saya! This robot looks like a woman. Saya wears clothes and has long, dark hair. Her rubber skin looks real. She can even smile, frown, and show anger on her face.

4   Saya was tested in an elementary school classroom in Japan. During the test, Saya took attendance. She said things like "Thank you," and told noisy kids to be quiet. The students enjoyed the robot.

5   "Robots that look human tend to be a big hit with young children," says Japanese scientist Hiroshi Kobayashi. He created Saya.

Looking Ahead

6   In the future, classroom robots will be able to do much more. But experts say robots will never be able to do all the things that human teachers can.

7   "A robot is just a tool," says Kobayashi.

Students with Saya

Name: _____

Directions: Read the article "Teaching Machines." Then answer the questions below.

1. What is the article mostly about?

   A. The history of robots

   B. How robots are built

   C. How robots are helping teachers in the classroom

   D. How robots will one day take the place of humans

2. Read the following sentences from paragraph 2.

> In South Korea, learning English is important.
> But there are not enough English teachers.

What is the most likely reason the author includes these sentences?

   A. To show how language robots are helping solve an important problem in South Korea

   B. To prove that English is the most important subject in South Korean schools

   C. To compare English teachers in Japan with those in South Korea

   D. To explain why becoming a teacher in South Korea is very difficult

3. What is the author's main point about Saya?

   A. Saya helps the teacher by taking attendance.

   B. Children prefer Saya over their human teacher.

   C. Saya is a better classroom robot than the robots in South Korea.

   D. Saya looks and acts like a human.

4. Which detail best supports your response in question 3?

   A. Saya wears clothes and has long, dark hair. *(paragraph 3)*

   B. Saya was tested in an elementary school classroom in Japan. *(paragraph 4)*

   C. In the future, classroom robots will be able to do much more. *(paragraph 6)*

   D. "A robot is just a tool," says Kobayashi. *(paragraph 7)*

5. How are the robot language teachers and Saya similar? How are they different? Explain.

_____

_____

_____

_____

_____

Teaching Machines

1 Do you have someone in your classroom who helps your teacher? In countries such as Japan and South Korea, some schools have robots to do just that.

Language Teachers

2 In South Korea, learning English is an important skill. But there are not enough English teachers. That's why some schools are using robots to help teach students how to speak English. These machines also read stories to the students in English. The South Korean government plans to add many more robots to their schools.

Say Hi to Saya

3 Most robots look like machines. Not Saya! This robot resembles a human woman. She was tested in an elementary school classroom in Japan.

4 Saya wears clothes and has long, dark hair. Her rubber skin looks real. The robot can even smile, frown, and show anger on her face.

5 During the test, Saya showed that she can take attendance, say things like "Thank you," and tell noisy kids to be quiet. The students enjoyed the robot.

6 "Robots that look human tend to be a big hit with young children," says Japanese scientist Hiroshi Kobayashi. He created Saya.

Looking Ahead

7 In the future, classroom robots will be able to do much more. But experts say that robots will never be able to do all the things that human teachers can.

8 "A robot is just a tool," says Kobayashi.

Students with Saya

Name: _____

Directions: Read the article "Teaching Machines."
Then answer the questions below.

1. What is the article mostly about?

    A. How robots are built

    B. The history of robots

    C. How robots will one day take the place of humans

    D. How robots are helping teachers in the classroom

2. Read the following sentences from paragraph 2.

> In South Korea, learning English is an important skill.
> But there are not enough English teachers.

  What is the most likely reason the author includes these sentences?

    A. To prove that English is the most important subject in South Korean schools

    B. To show how language robots are helping solve an important problem in South Korea

    C. To compare English teachers in Japan with those in South Korea

    D. To explain why becoming a teacher in South Korea is very difficult

3. What is the author's main point about Saya?

    A. Children prefer Saya over their human teacher.

    B. Saya looks and acts like a human.

    C. Saya is a better classroom robot than the robots in South Korea.

    D. Saya helps the teacher by taking attendance.

4. Which detail best supports your response in question 3?

    A. "A robot is just a tool," says Kobayashi. *(paragraph 8)*

    B. In the future, classroom robots will be able to do much more. *(paragraph 7)*

    C. She was tested in an elementary school classroom in Japan. *(paragraph 3)*

    D. Saya wears clothes and has long, dark hair. *(paragraph 4)*

5. How are the robot language teachers and Saya similar? How are they different? Explain.

_____

_____

_____

_____

_____

Teaching Machines

1   Do you have someone in your classroom who helps your teacher? In countries such as Japan and South Korea, some schools have robots to assist teachers.

Language Teachers

2   In South Korea, learning English is an important skill, but there are not enough English teachers. That's why some schools are using robots to help teach students how to speak English. These machines also read stories to the students in English. The South Korean government plans to add many more robots to their schools.

Say Hi to Saya

3   Most robots look like machines, but not Saya! This robot resembles a human woman. She was tested in an elementary school classroom in Japan.

4   Saya wears clothes and has long, dark hair. Her rubber skin looks real. The robot can even display emotions. She can smile, frown, and show anger on her face.

5   During the test, Saya showed that she can take attendance, say things like "Thank you," and tell noisy kids to be quiet. The students enjoyed the robot.

6   "Robots that look human tend to be a big hit with young children," says Japanese scientist Hiroshi Kobayashi, who created Saya.

Looking Ahead

7   In the future, classroom robots will be able to do much more. But experts say that robots will never be able to do all the things that human teachers can.

8   "A robot is just a tool," says Kobayashi.

Students with Saya

Name: _____

Directions: Read the article "Teaching Machines."
Then answer the questions below.

1. What is the article mostly about?

    A. How robots will one day take the place of humans

    B. How robots are helping teachers in the classroom

    C. How robots are built

    D. The history of robots

2. Read the following sentence from paragraph 2.

> In South Korea, learning English is an important skill,
> but there are not enough English teachers.

What is the most likely reason the author includes this sentence?

    A. To explain why becoming a teacher in South Korea is very difficult

    B. To compare English teachers in Japan with those in South Korea

    C. To prove that English is the most important subject in South Korean schools

    D. To show how language robots are helping solve an important problem in South Korea

3. What is the author's main point about Saya?

    A. Saya looks and acts like a human.

    B. Children prefer Saya over their human teacher.

    C. Saya is a better classroom robot than the robots in South Korea.

    D. Saya helps the teacher by taking attendance.

4. Which detail best supports your response in question 3?

    A. In the future, classroom robots will be able to do much more. *(paragraph 7)*

    B. Saya wears clothes and has long, dark hair. *(paragraph 4)*

    C. "A robot is just a tool," says Kobayashi. *(paragraph 8)*

    D. She was tested in an elementary school classroom in Japan. *(paragraph 3)*

5. How are the robot language teachers and Saya similar? How are they different? Explain.

_____

_____

_____

_____

_____

Seal Rescue

1   Picture this: A baby seal snoozes on a beach in Seattle. Its mom is out fishing for food in the water. It's a peaceful day for this seal family—but not for long. Suddenly, people on the beach rush over to the seal pup. They want to get a closer look at it. Some try to feed or pet it.

2   The pup is now scared. And the mom, looking on from the waves, is just as frightened.

3   "If people crowd around the pup, the mother might be too afraid to come back for her baby," explains Noemi Reche-Ley. Noemi is a student volunteer for a group called Seal Sitters. They help keep seal pups living near the shore safe from people.

Beach Babysitters

4   Noemi and other volunteers find sleeping seal pups on the beach. They close off the areas around the pups with yellow tape. Then they stand guard from about 100 yards away. They watch over the pups with binoculars. If people try to get near the pups, the Seal Sitters stop them. They explain to the people why the seals shouldn't be disturbed.

5   One big reason is that seal pups really need their moms. Like most baby mammals, seal pups rely on their mothers' milk. It has the nutrients they need to survive. If the babies are kept apart from their moms, they are likely to die.

6   Seals are also threatened by pollution. People sometimes leave garbage, such as plastic bags, on the beach. Noemi and the group try to keep the beach clean. They don't want the animals swallowing things that could make them sick.

7   "I love seals," says Noemi, "and I want to protect them."

WORDS TO KNOW
nutrients: vitamins an animal or plant needs to live
pollution: harmful substances in the environment

A seal pup on its own

Name: _____

Directions: Read the article "Seal Rescue." Then answer the questions below.

1. **Which choice best describes the article's main idea?**

   A. Seals are peaceful animals.

   B. Mother seals will not come back for their pups if they are afraid.

   C. A group of volunteers helps seal pups stay safe on the beach.

   D. People are interested in getting a close look at baby seals.

2. **What is the purpose of the story the author tells in the beginning of the article?**

   A. To describe how a seal catches its food

   B. To explain what can happen when humans get too close to baby seals

   C. To describe how the author fed and petted a baby seal

   D. To show how dangerous seals can be to humans

3. **What is most likely to happen if a baby seal is kept away from its mom?**

   A. It will not get the food it needs to stay alive.

   B. It will go in the water to try to find its mom.

   C. It will swallow garbage that could make it sick.

   D. It will be too afraid to go in the water alone.

4. **According to the article, which do Seal Sitters do first?**

   A. Block off the area around a seal pup

   B. Look for sleeping seal pups

   C. Explain to people why it's important to leave seal pups alone

   D. Watch over seal pups from far away

5. **Name one way humans can hurt seals and one way humans can help them. Use details from the article.**

Way humans can hurt seals	Way humans can help seals

Seal Rescue

1   Picture this: A baby seal snoozes on a beach in Seattle. Its mom is out fishing for food in the water. It's a peaceful day for this seal family—but not for long. Suddenly, people on the beach rush over to the seal pup to get a closer look at it. Some try to feed or pet it.

2   The pup is now scared—and the mom, looking on from the waves, is just as frightened.

3   "If people crowd around the pup, the mother might be too afraid to come back for her baby," explains Noemi Reche-Ley. Noemi is a student volunteer for a group called Seal Sitters. They help keep seal pups living near the shore safe from people.

Beach Babysitters

4   Noemi and other volunteers find sleeping seal pups and close off the areas around them with yellow tape. Then they stand guard from about 100 yards away and watch over the pups with binoculars. If people try to get near the pups, the Seal Sitters stop them and explain to them why the seals shouldn't be disturbed.

5   One big reason is that seal pups really need their moms. Like most baby mammals, seal pups rely on their mothers' milk. It has the nutrients they need to survive. If the babies are kept apart from their moms, they are likely to die.

6   Seals are also threatened by pollution. People sometimes leave garbage, such as plastic bags, on the beach. Noemi and the group try to keep the beach clean. They don't want the animals swallowing things that could make them sick.

7   "I love seals," says Noemi, "and I want to protect them."

WORDS TO KNOW
nutrients: vitamins an animal or plant needs to live
pollution: harmful substances in the environment

A seal pup on its own

Name: _____

Directions: Read the article "Seal Rescue." Then answer the questions below.

1. **Which choice best describes the article's main idea?**
   A. A group of volunteers helps seal pups stay safe on the beach.
   B. Mother seals will not come back for their pups if they are afraid.
   C. People are interested in getting a close look at baby seals.
   D. Seals are peaceful animals.

2. **According to the article, which do Seal Sitters do first?**
   A. Block off the area around a seal pup
   B. Explain to people why it's important to leave seal pups alone
   C. Look for sleeping seal pups
   D. Watch over seal pups from far away

3. **What is the purpose of the story the author tells in the beginning of the article?**
   A. To describe how the author fed and petted a baby seal
   B. To show how dangerous seals can be to humans
   C. To describe how a seal catches its food
   D. To explain what can happen when humans get too close to baby seals

4. **What is most likely to happen if a baby seal is kept away from its mom?**
   A. It will go in the water to try to find its mom.
   B. It will be too afraid to go in the water alone.
   C. It will swallow garbage that could make it sick.
   D. It will not get the food it needs to stay alive.

5. **Name two ways humans can hurt seals and two ways humans can help them. Use details from the article.**

Ways humans can hurt seals	Ways humans can help seals
1.	1.
2.	2.

Seal Rescue

1   Picture this: A baby seal snoozes on a beach in Seattle. Its mom is out fishing for food in the water. It's a peaceful day for this seal family—but not for long. Suddenly, people on the beach rush over to the seal pup to get a closer look at it. Some try to feed or pet it.

2   The pup is now scared—and its mom, looking on from the waves, is just as frightened.

3   "If people crowd around the pup, the mother might be too afraid to come back for her baby," explains Noemi Reche-Ley, a student volunteer for a group called Seal Sitters. They help keep people away from seal pups living near the shore.

Beach Babysitters

4   Noemi and other volunteers find sleeping seal pups and close off the areas around them with yellow tape. Then they stand guard from about 100 yards away, keeping a close eye over the pups with binoculars. If people try to get near the pups, the Seal Sitters stop them and explain to them why the seals shouldn't be disturbed.

5   One big reason is that seal pups really need their moms. Like most baby mammals, seal pups rely on their mothers' milk, which is rich in nutrients they need to survive. If the babies are kept apart from their moms, they may likely die of starvation.

6   Seals are also threatened by pollution. People sometimes leave garbage, such as plastic bags, on the beach. Noemi and the group try to keep the beach clean. They don't want the animals swallowing things that could make them sick.

7   "I love seals," says Noemi, "and I want to protect them."

WORDS TO KNOW

nutrients: vitamins needed by an animal or plant to live

pollution: harmful substances in the environment

A seal pup on its own

Directions: Read the article "Seal Rescue." Then answer the questions below.

1. Which choice best describes the article's main idea?

    A. People are interested in getting a close look at baby seals.

    B. Seals are peaceful animals.

    C. Mother seals will not come back for their pups if they are afraid.

    D. A group of volunteers helps seal pups stay safe on the beach.

2. What is the purpose of the story the author tells in the beginning of the article?

    A. To show how dangerous seals can be to humans

    B. To describe how the author fed and petted a baby seal

    C. To describe how a seal catches its food

    D. To explain what can happen when humans get too close to baby seals

3. According to the article, which do Seal Sitters do first?

    A. Watch over seal pups from far away

    B. Explain to people why it's important to leave seal pups alone

    C. Look for sleeping seal pups

    D. Block off the area around a seal pup

4. What is most likely to happen if a baby seal is kept away from its mom?

    A. It will not get the food it needs to stay alive.

    B. It will go in the water to try to find its mom.

    C. It will be too afraid to go in the water alone.

    D. It will swallow garbage that could make it sick.

5. Identify two ways humans can hurt seals and two ways humans can help them. Use details from the article.

Ways humans can hurt seals	Ways humans can help seals
1.	1.
2.	2.

I Survived a Tornado

1   Tornadoes can appear suddenly without warning. They can toss trucks and cars in their path. They can also destroy buildings. They are one of the most powerful forces of nature on Earth. More than 1,000 tornadoes form in the United States every year.

2   Logan knows what it's like to face a tornado. He lives in a town named Phil Campbell in Alabama. A twister with winds of more than 200 miles per hour smashed into his house.

Twister Trouble

3   It had been just a regular day for Logan and his family. Then the power in their house went out. They didn't know a tornado was heading straight for their town. Logan's grandmother called to warn them. A news report said the tornado was minutes away.

4   Logan and his family could hear the storm coming. "We heard a loud rumbling," Logan told *Scholastic News*. "All of a sudden, the walls started shaking."

5   Logan had never experienced a tornado before. But his teacher had told his class what to do in case one was coming.

6   "She taught me to get in the bathroom or the basement," he said. "My family jumped in the basement."

After the Storm

7   After the tornado passed, Logan saw the damage it had caused. "All of the trees were down," recalled Logan. "Our whole living room, the garage, and part of our kitchen were gone."

8   Today, Logan and his family live in a new house in the same town. He says it's been hard getting used to living in a new home. But life is slowly returning to normal. "It was kind of tough for a while," he said. "But things are OK now."

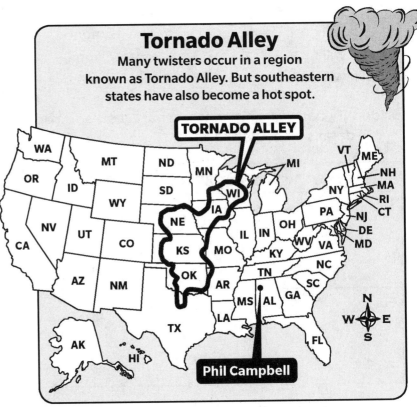

Tornado Alley

Many twisters occur in a region known as Tornado Alley. But southeastern states have also become a hot spot.

TORNADO ALLEY

Phil Campbell

Name: _____

Directions: Read the article "I Survived a Tornado" and study the map. Then answer the questions below.

1. **Which word in the article means the same as *tornado*?**

    A. Nature

    B. Twister

    C. Experienced

    D. Damage

2. **Which sentence best summarizes the main idea of the section "Twister Trouble"?**

    A. Logan's family could hear the storm approaching.

    B. Logan's grandmother warned his family that a tornado was coming.

    C. Logan's family found out about the tornado just in time to take shelter in the basement.

    D. Logan had never experienced a tornado before.

3. **Explain how the tornado affected Logan and his family. Use one detail from the article to support your answer.**

    _____

    _____

    _____

    _____

4. **How does the map add to the reader's knowledge of tornadoes in the United States? Use one detail from the map that is not included in the article.**

    _____

    _____

    _____

    _____

I Survived a Tornado

1   Tornadoes can appear suddenly and without warning. As they move across the land, they can toss trucks and cars. They can also destroy buildings. They are one of the most powerful and **destructive** forces of nature on Earth. In the United States, more than 1,000 tornadoes form every year.

2   Logan knows what it's like to face a tornado. He lives in a town named Phil Campbell in Alabama. A twister with winds of more than 200 miles per hour smashed into his house.

Twister Trouble

3   It had been just a regular day for Logan and his family. Then the power in their house went out. They didn't know that a tornado was heading straight for their town. But Logan's grandmother called to warn them. A news report said that the tornado was minutes away.

4   Logan and his family could hear the storm coming. "We heard a loud rumbling," Logan told *Scholastic News*. "All of a sudden, the walls started shaking."

5   Logan had never experienced a tornado before. But his teacher had told his class what to do in case one was coming.

6   "She taught me to get in the hallway and duck down or get in the bathroom or the basement," he said. "My family jumped in the basement."

After the Storm

7   After the tornado passed, Logan saw the damage it had caused. "All of the trees were down," recalled Logan. "Our whole living room, the garage, and part of our kitchen were gone."

8   Today, Logan and his family live in a new house in the same town. He says it's been hard getting used to living in a new home. But life is slowly returning to normal. "It was kind of tough for a while," he said. "But things are OK now."

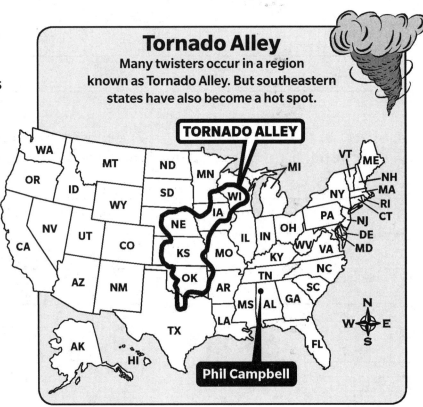

Tornado Alley

Many twisters occur in a region known as Tornado Alley. But southeastern states have also become a hot spot.

TORNADO ALLEY

Phil Campbell

Name: _____

Directions: Read the article "I Survived a Tornado" and study the map. Then answer the questions below.

1. Read this sentence from paragraph 1.

> They are one of the most powerful and **destructive** forces of nature on Earth.

Which word is most similar in meaning to *destructive*?
   A. Damaging
   B. Helpful
   C. Weak
   D. Windy

2. Which sentence best summarizes the main idea of the section "Twister Trouble"?
   A. Logan had never experienced a tornado before.
   B. Logan's family found out about the tornado just in time to take shelter in the basement.
   C. Logan's grandmother warned his family that a tornado was coming.
   D. Logan's family could hear the storm approaching.

3. Explain how the tornado affected Logan and his family. Use two details from the article to support your answer.

_____

_____

_____

_____

4. Explain how the map adds to the reader's knowledge of tornadoes in the United States. Use two details from the map that are not included in the article.

_____

_____

_____

_____

I Survived a Tornado

1   Tornadoes can appear suddenly, without warning. And they can't be stopped. As they move across the land, they can toss trucks and cars, and **demolish** buildings. They are one of the most powerful and destructive forces of nature on Earth. In the United States, more than 1,000 tornadoes form per year on average.

2   Logan, a young boy living in a town named Phil Campbell, Alabama, knows what it's like to face a tornado. A twister with winds of more than 200 miles per hour smashed into his house.

Twister Trouble

3   The day had started out just like any regular day for Logan and his family. Then the power in their house went out. Little did they know that a tornado was heading straight for their town. But then Logan's grandmother called to warn them. A news report said that the tornado was minutes away.

4   Logan and his family could hear the storm approaching. "We heard a loud rumbling," Logan told *Scholastic News*. "All of a sudden, the walls started shaking."

5   Logan had never experienced a tornado before. But his teacher had told his class what to do in case one was coming.

6   "She taught me to get in the hallway and duck down or get in the bathroom or the basement," he says. "My family jumped in the basement."

After the Storm

7   Once the tornado passed, Logan couldn't believe the damage it had caused. "All of the trees were down," recalls Logan. "Our whole living room, the garage, and part of our kitchen were gone."

8   Today, Logan and his family live in a new house in the same town. He says it's been hard getting used to living in a new home, but life is slowly returning to normal. "It was kind of tough for a while," he said. "But things are OK now."

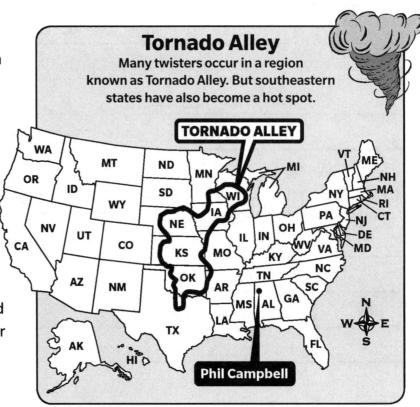

Tornado Alley

Many twisters occur in a region known as Tornado Alley. But southeastern states have also become a hot spot.

Name: _____

Directions: Read the article "I Survived a Tornado" and study the map. Then answer the questions below.

1. Read this sentence from paragraph 1.

> As they move across the land, they can toss trucks and cars, and **demolish** buildings.

Which word is most similar in meaning to *demolish*?

A. Warn

B. Toss

C. Destroy

D. Restore

2. Which sentence best summarizes the main idea of the section "Twister Trouble"?

A. Logan's grandmother warned his family that a tornado was coming.

B. Logan's family could hear the storm approaching.

C. Logan had never experienced a tornado before.

D. Logan's family found out about the tornado just in time to take shelter in the basement.

3. Explain how the tornado affected Logan and his family. Use two details from the article to support your answer.

_____

_____

_____

_____

4. Explain how the map adds to the reader's knowledge of tornadoes in the United States. Use two details from the map that are not included in the article.

_____

_____

_____

_____

Tracking Turtles

1   It happens every summer on beaches in Florida and nearby states. Thousands of loggerhead sea turtles hatch from their eggs. The baby turtles are only a little bigger than a quarter. They race into the Atlantic Ocean and swim away.

2   But where do they go? Scientist Kate Mansfield wanted to know. "I've always wondered what happens to these little guys," she says. She and other scientists set out to solve the mystery.

Ocean Detectives

3   Mansfield and her team gathered 17 baby loggerheads. When the babies grew strong enough, the scientists stuck small computers on their shells. Then they released the turtles into the ocean. The computers recorded **data** about each turtle's trip.

4   The scientists were surprised by some of the information they learned. They thought the babies would follow the Atlantic Ocean currents. These currents move in a big circle. But many of the babies swam out of the currents. They went to a spot in the center of the circle. This area has thick patches of seaweed. The turtles climbed aboard and floated on them.

Safe in the Seaweed

5   Mansfield says that heading for seaweed patches makes sense. They are perfect places for baby turtles to grow up. The turtles can hide from sharks. They can soak up the sun to stay warm. They can also gobble up bugs and other creatures that live there. Before long, the turtles grow to be bigger than dinner plates!

6   When they are a few years old, the sea turtles move closer to shore. And once they're adults, many females return to the beaches where they were born. They lay their eggs there. Soon, a new batch of turtles will make their way out to the seaweed.

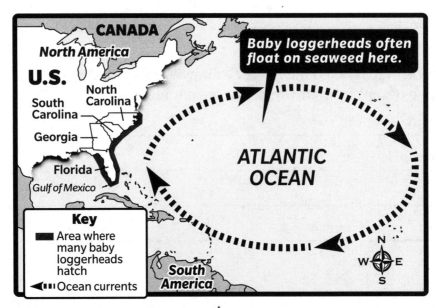

CANADA
North America
U.S.
North Carolina
South Carolina
Georgia
Florida
Gulf of Mexico
South America
ATLANTIC OCEAN

Baby loggerheads often float on seaweed here.

Key
Area where many baby loggerheads hatch
Ocean currents

Name: _____

Directions: Read the article "Tracking Turtles." Then answer the questions below.

1. What is the main idea of the article "Tracking Turtles"?

    A. Loggerhead sea turtles hatch from eggs.

    B. Scientists have learned where baby loggerhead sea turtles go.

    C. Computers can teach scientists a lot about different animals.

    D. Scientists don't know why the Atlantic Ocean currents move in a circle.

2. Which detail from the article best supports the answer to question 1?

    A. It happens every summer on beaches in Florida and nearby states. *(paragraph 1)*

    B. They went to a spot in the center of the circle. *(paragraph 4)*

    C. Before long, the turtles grow to be bigger than dinner plates! *(paragraph 5)*

    D. These currents move in a big circle. *(paragraph 4)*

3. In paragraph 1, the author uses the phrase "race into" to show that _____.

    A. the turtles are competing in a race

    B. turtles in Florida are slow

    C. the turtles are rushing to get to the water

    D. the turtles are escaping danger

4. What does the word *data* mean as it is used in paragraph 3 of the article?

    A. Computers

    B. Movements

    C. Facts

    D. Mysteries

5. Which detail from the article best supports the answer to question 4?

    A. The scientists were surprised by some of the information they learned. *(paragraph 4)*

    B. She and other scientists set out to solve the mystery. *(paragraph 2)*

    C. This area has thick patches of seaweed. *(paragraph 4)*

    D. When they are a few years old, the sea turtles move closer to shore. *(paragraph 6)*

6. Which inference can you make from the article?

    A. Seaweed is a sea turtle's favorite food.

    B. Bug bites are dangerous for sea turtles.

    C. Sea turtles try to stay out of the sun.

    D. Sharks have been known to eat sea turtles.

Name: _____

7. Kate Mansfield and the other scientists were surprised by what they learned. Which detail from the article best supports this idea?

    A. Mansfield and her team gathered 17 baby loggerheads. *(paragraph 3)*

    B. They thought the babies would follow the Atlantic Ocean currents. *(paragraph 4)*

    C. The turtles can hide from sharks. *(paragraph 5)*

    D. The baby turtles are only a little bigger than a quarter. *(paragraph 1)*

8. Which detail does the map not show?

    A. Where Mansfield and her team work

    B. Where the baby loggerheads hatch

    C. In which direction the ocean currents move

    D. Where the baby loggerheads go after they hatch

Tracking Turtles

1   It happens every summer on beaches in Florida and nearby states. Thousands of loggerhead sea turtles hatch from their eggs. The baby turtles are only a little bigger than a quarter. They race into the Atlantic Ocean and swim away.

2   But where do they go? Scientist Kate Mansfield wanted to know. "I've always wondered what happens to these little guys," she says. She and other scientists set out to solve the mystery.

Ocean Detectives

3   Mansfield and her team gathered 17 baby loggerheads. When the babies grew strong enough, the scientists stuck small computers on their shells. Then they released the turtles into the ocean. The computers recorded **data** about each turtle's trip.

4   The scientists were surprised by some of the information they learned. They thought the babies would follow the Atlantic Ocean currents. These currents move in a big circle. But many of the babies swam out of the currents and went to a spot in the center of the circle. This area has thick patches of seaweed. The turtles climbed aboard and floated on them.

Safe in the Seaweed

5   Mansfield says that heading for seaweed patches makes sense. They are perfect places for baby turtles to grow up. The turtles can hide from sharks and soak up the sun to stay warm. They can also gobble up bugs and other creatures that live there. Before long, the turtles grow to be bigger than dinner plates!

6   When they are a few years old, the sea turtles migrate, or travel, closer to shore. And once they're adults, many females return to the beaches where they were born to lay eggs. Soon, a new batch of turtles will make their way out to the seaweed.

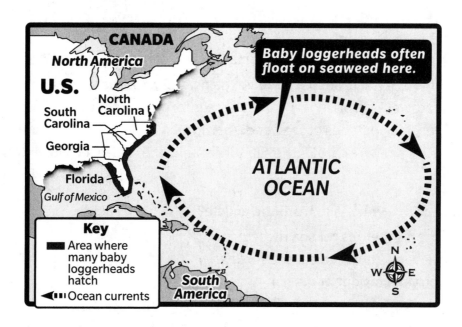

CANADA
North America
U.S.
North Carolina
South Carolina
Georgia
Florida
Gulf of Mexico
South America

Baby loggerheads often float on seaweed here.

ATLANTIC OCEAN

N
W E
S

Key
Area where many baby loggerheads hatch
Ocean currents

Name: _____

Directions: Read the article "Tracking Turtles." Then answer the questions below.

1. **What is the main idea of the article "Tracking Turtles"?**
    A. Loggerhead sea turtles hatch from eggs in the summer.
    B. Computers can teach scientists a lot about different animals.
    C. Scientists have learned where baby loggerhead sea turtles go.
    D. It's a mystery why the Atlantic Ocean currents move in a circle.

2. **Which detail from the article best supports the answer to question 1?**
    A. It happens every summer on beaches in Florida and nearby states. (*paragraph 1*)
    B. These currents move in a big circle. (*paragraph 4*)
    C. But many of the babies swam out of the currents and went to a spot in the center of the circle. (*paragraph 4*)
    D. Before long, the turtles grow to be bigger than dinner plates! (*paragraph 5*)

3. **In paragraph 1, the author uses the phrase "race into" to show that _____.**
    A. turtles in Florida are slow
    B. the turtles are competing in a race
    C. the turtles are escaping danger
    D. the turtles are rushing to get to the water

4. **What does the word *data* mean as it is used in paragraph 3 of the article?**
    A. Facts
    B. Mysteries
    C. Computers
    D. Movements

5. **Which detail from the article best supports the answer to question 4?**
    A. She and other scientists set out to solve the mystery. (*paragraph 2*)
    B. The scientists were surprised by some of the information they learned. (*paragraph 4*)
    C. This area has thick patches of seaweed. (*paragraph 4*)
    D. When they are a few years old, the sea turtles migrate, or travel, closer to shore. (*paragraph 6*)

6. **Which inference can you make from the article?**
    A. Bug bites are dangerous for sea turtles.
    B. Sharks have been known to eat sea turtles.
    C. Sea turtles try to stay out of the sun.
    D. Seaweed is a sea turtle's favorite food.

Name: _____

7. Kate Mansfield and the other scientists were surprised by what they learned. Which detail from the article best supports this idea?

    A. The baby turtles are only a little bigger than a quarter. *(paragraph 1)*

    B. Mansfield and her team gathered 17 baby loggerheads. *(paragraph 3)*

    C. They thought the babies would follow the Atlantic Ocean currents. *(paragraph 4)*

    D. The turtles can hide from sharks and soak up the sun to stay warm. *(paragraph 5)*

8. Scientists discovered that young loggerhead sea turtles migrate to the center of the Atlantic's circular currents. Why might baby turtles do this, according to the article? Use details from the article to support your answer.

_____

_____

_____

_____

_____

_____

Tracking Turtles

1   Every summer on beaches in Florida and nearby states, thousands of loggerhead sea turtles hatch from their eggs. The baby turtles are only a little bigger than a quarter. They race into the Atlantic Ocean and swim away.

2   But where do they go? Scientist Kate Mansfield wanted to know. "I've always wondered what happens to these little guys," she says. She and other scientists set out to solve the mystery.

Ocean Detectives

3   Mansfield and her team gathered 17 baby loggerheads. When the babies grew strong enough, the scientists stuck small computers on their shells and then released them into the ocean. The computers recorded **data** about each turtle's trip.

4   The scientists were surprised by some of the information they learned. They thought the babies would follow the Atlantic Ocean currents, which move in a big circle. But many of the babies swam out of the currents and went to a spot in the center of the circle. This area has thick patches of seaweed. The turtles climbed aboard and floated on them.

Safe in the Seaweed

5   Mansfield says that heading for seaweed patches makes sense. They are perfect places for baby turtles to grow up. The turtles can hide from sharks and soak up the sun to stay warm. They can also gobble up bugs and other creatures that live there. Before long, the turtles grow to be bigger than dinner plates!

6   When they are a few years old, the sea turtles migrate, or travel, closer to shore. And once they're adults, many females return to the beaches where they were born to lay eggs. Soon, a new batch of turtles will make their way out to the seaweed.

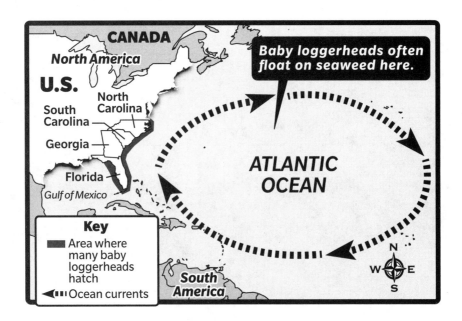

Baby loggerheads often float on seaweed here.

CANADA
North America
U.S.
North Carolina
South Carolina
Georgia
Florida
Gulf of Mexico
ATLANTIC OCEAN
South America

Key
Area where many baby loggerheads hatch
Ocean currents

Name: _____

Directions: Read the article "Tracking Turtles." Then answer the questions below.

1. What is the main idea of the article "Tracking Turtles"?

    A. Computers can teach scientists a lot about different animals.

    B. Loggerhead sea turtles hatch from eggs in the summer.

    C. It's a mystery why the Atlantic Ocean currents move in a circle.

    D. Scientists have learned where baby loggerhead sea turtles go.

2. Which detail from the article best supports the answer to question 1?

    A. They thought the babies would follow the Atlantic Ocean currents, which move in a big circle. *(paragraph 4)*

    B. Every summer on beaches in Florida and nearby states, thousands of loggerhead sea turtles hatch from their eggs. *(paragraph 1)*

    C. Before long, the turtles grow to be bigger than dinner plates! *(paragraph 5)*

    D. But many of the babies swam out of the currents and went to a spot in the center of the circle. *(paragraph 4)*

3. In paragraph 1, the author uses the phrase "race into" to show that _____.

    A. the turtles are competing in a race

    B. the turtles are rushing to get to the water

    C. turtles in Florida are slow

    D. the turtles are escaping danger

4. What does the word *data* mean as it is used in paragraph 3 of the article?

    A. Computers

    B. Facts

    C. Mysteries

    D. Movements

5. Which detail from the article best supports the answer to question 4?

    A. This area has thick patches of seaweed. *(paragraph 4)*

    B. She and other scientists set out to solve the mystery. *(paragraph 2)*

    C. When they are a few years old, the sea turtles migrate, or travel, closer to shore. *(paragraph 6)*

    D. The scientists were surprised by some of the information they learned. *(paragraph 4)*

Name: _____

6. Which inference can you make from the article?

    A. Sharks have been known to eat sea turtles.

    B. Bug bites are dangerous for sea turtles.

    C. Seaweed is a sea turtle's favorite food.

    D. Sea turtles try to stay out of the sun.

7. Kate Mansfield and the other scientists were surprised by what they learned. Which detail from the article best supports this idea?

    A. The baby turtles are only a little bigger than a quarter. *(paragraph 1)*

    B. Mansfield and her team gathered 17 baby loggerheads. *(paragraph 3)*

    C. They thought the babies would follow the Atlantic Ocean currents, which move in a big circle. *(paragraph 4)*

    D. The turtles can hide from sharks and soak up the sun to stay warm. *(paragraph 5)*

8. Scientists discovered that young loggerhead sea turtles migrate to the center of the Atlantic's circular currents. Why might baby turtles do this, according to the article? Use details from the article to support your answer.

_____

_____

_____

_____

_____

_____

Furry Friends

1   It was a sunny day in Georgia. Three animals played together on a field of grass. That may not sound strange. But this group of animal friends was really special. It was made up of a tiger, a bear, and a lion!

2   These animals made surprising friends. For one thing, each animal came from a different part of the world. They're also all top hunters. They most likely wouldn't get along in the wild.

3   "They would probably fight over food [in the wild]," says Kandi Allen. She works at Noah's Ark. The Ark is a **sanctuary**—a safe home for animals that have been hurt or abused.

A Sad Past

4   The tiger is called Shere Khan (sher KON), and the bear is Baloo. The lion's name was Leo. Leo passed away in 2016. But the three animals had lived together for 15 years.

5   When they were cubs, the animals were found in a basement in Georgia. Their owners had bought the cubs to keep as pets. That's against the law. They also did not take good care of the animals. So the furry friends were rescued. They were brought to Noah's Ark.

A Wild Lesson

6   At Noah's Ark, the animals had much more room. The outdoor space is about the size of three football fields. For years, the animals played, slept, and ate together there.

7   Shere Khan, Baloo, and Leo couldn't be returned to the wild. That's because they were raised by humans. They wouldn't be able to survive without human help. Workers at Noah's Ark tell visitors that animals like tigers, bears, and lions don't make good pets. "Wild animals belong in the wild," says Allen.

MEET THE CREATURES			
Name	**Type of Animal**	**Weight**	**Natural Habitat**
Shere Khan	Bengal tiger	350 pounds	Asia
Baloo	American black bear	700 pounds	North America
Leo	Lion	500 pounds	Africa

Name: _____

Directions: Read the article "Furry Friends." Then answer the questions below.

1. Which of the following sentences best states the main idea of the article?

  A. Tigers, bears, and lions make good pets.

  B. Surprisingly, a tiger, a bear, and a lion became good friends.

  C. It is against the law in Georgia to keep wild animals as pets.

  D. Tigers, bears, and lions come from different parts of the world.

2. What is the meaning of the word *sanctuary* as it is used in the article?

  A. A crate where a pet animal might be kept

  B. A football field or other grassy area

  C. A place where animals are protected

  D. A person who cares for wild animals

3. What inference about baby tigers, bears, and lions can you make from the article?

  A. They are all called cubs.

  B. They all make good pets.

  C. They all come from Africa.

  D. They are all about the same size.

4. Which sentence from the article best supports the answer to question 3?

  A. But this group of animal friends was really special. *(paragraph 1)*

  B. When they were cubs, the animals were found in a basement in Georgia. *(paragraph 5)*

  C. So the furry friends were rescued. *(paragraph 5)*

  D. They're also all top hunters. *(paragraph 2)*

5. Why couldn't the three animals be returned to the wild?

  A. They were raised by humans and couldn't survive without human help.

  B. They have a very close bond and couldn't survive without each other.

  C. They sometimes do not get along.

  D. They don't make good pets.

6. Which is the most likely reason that the author includes the chart "Meet the Creatures"?

  A. To show what each animal friend looks like

  B. To describe how the three animal friends spend their days

  C. To explain how people care for the three animal friends

  D. To compare and contrast the three animal friends

Name: _____

7. Why is the friendship among Shere Khan, Baloo, and Leo surprising?
   Use details from the article to support your answer.

_____

_____

_____

_____

_____

_____

_____

_____

_____

_____

Leo   Baloo   Shere Khan

Furry Friends

1   It was a sunny day in Georgia. Three animals played and cuddled on a stretch of grass. That may not sound strange. But this group of animal friends was really special. It was made up of a tiger, a bear, and a lion!

2   These animals made surprising pals. One reason is that they each came from different parts of the world. They're also all top predators, or hunters. They most likely wouldn't get along in the wild.

3   "If they ever did meet up in the wild, they would probably fight over food," says Kandi Allen. She works at Noah's Ark. The Ark is a **sanctuary**—a safe home for animals that have been hurt or abused.

A Sad Past

4   The tiger is called Shere Khan (sher KON), and the bear is Baloo. The lion's name was Leo. Leo passed away in 2016. But the three animals had lived together for 15 years.

5   When the three creatures were cubs, they were found in a basement in Georgia. Their owners had bought the cubs to keep as pets. That's against the law. They had not taken good care of the cubs. The furry pals were rescued and brought to the sanctuary. Finally, they would have a safe place to live.

A Wild Lesson

6   At the sanctuary, the animals had much more room to roam around. The outdoor space at Noah's Ark is about the size of three football fields. For years, the animals played, slept, and ate together there. They even groomed each other.

7   Shere Khan, Baloo, and Leo couldn't be returned to the wild. That's because they were raised by humans. They wouldn't be able to survive without human help. Workers at Noah's Ark always remind visitors that animals like tigers, bears, and lions don't make good pets. "Wild animals belong in the wild," says Allen.

MEET THE CREATURES			
Name	Type of Animal	Weight	Natural Habitat
Shere Khan	Bengal tiger	350 pounds	Asia
Baloo	American black bear	700 pounds	North America
Leo	Lion	500 pounds	Africa

Name: _____

Directions: Read the article "Furry Friends." Then answer the questions below.

1. Which of the following sentences best states the main idea of the article?

   A. It is against the law in Georgia to keep wild animals as pets.

   B. Tigers, bears, and lions come from different parts of the world.

   C. Surprisingly, a tiger, a bear, and a lion became good friends.

   D. Tigers, bears, and lions make good pets.

2. What is the meaning of the word _sanctuary_ as it is used in the article?

   A. An area where animals are protected

   B. A crate where a pet animal might be kept

   C. A person who cares for wild animals

   D. A football field or other grassy area

3. Which sentence from the article best supports the answer to question 2?

   A. That may not sound strange. (_paragraph 1_)

   B. Finally, they would have a safe place to live. (_paragraph 5_)

   C. They had not taken good care of the cubs. (_paragraph 5_)

   D. Three animals played and cuddled on a stretch of grass. (_paragraph 1_)

4. What inference about baby tigers, bears, and lions can you make from the article?

   A. They all make good pets.

   B. They are all about the same size.

   C. They are all called cubs.

   D. They all come from Africa.

5. Which sentence from the article best supports the answer to question 4?

   A. But this group of animal friends was really special. (_paragraph 1_)

   B. They're also all top predators, or hunters. (_paragraph 2_)

   C. The furry pals were rescued and brought to the sanctuary. (_paragraph 5_)

   D. When the three creatures were cubs, they were found in a basement in Georgia. (_paragraph 5_)

6. In paragraph 6, the author probably points out that the animals "even groomed each other" to show that they ____.

   A. have a very close bond

   B. sometimes do not get along

   C. could not survive in the wild

   D. do not have any humans to care for them

Name: _____

7. Which is the most likely reason that the author includes the chart "Meet the Creatures"?

    A. To explain how people care for the three animal friends

    B. To describe how the three animal friends spend their days

    C. To show what each animal friend looks like

    D. To compare and contrast the three animal friends

8. Why is the friendship among Shere Khan, Baloo, and Leo surprising, according to the article? Use details from the article to support your answer.

_____

_____

_____

_____

_____

_____

_____

_____

_____

_____

Leo   Baloo   Shere Khan

Furry Friends

1   It was a sunny day at an animal **sanctuary** in Georgia. Three creatures played and cuddled on a stretch of grass. That may not sound strange. But this group of animal friends was really special. It was made up of a tiger, a bear, and a lion!

2   These animals made surprising pals. One reason is that the three species came from different parts of the world. They're also all top predators, or hunters, that most likely wouldn't get along in the wild.

3   "If they ever did meet up in the wild, they would probably fight over food," says Kandi Allen. She works at the sanctuary, which is called Noah's Ark.

A Sad Past

4   The tiger is called Shere Khan (sher KON), and the bear is Baloo. The lion's name was Leo. Leo passed away in 2016. But the three animals had lived together for 15 years.

5   When the three creatures were cubs, they were found in a basement in Georgia. Their owners had bought the cubs to keep as pets even though that's against the law. They had not taken good care of the cubs. The furry pals were rescued and brought to the sanctuary. Finally, they would have a safe place to live.

A Wild Lesson

6   At the sanctuary, the animals had much more room to roam around. The outdoor space at Noah's Ark is about the size of three football fields. For years, the animals played, slept, and ate together there. They even groomed each other.

7   Shere Khan, Baloo, and Leo couldn't be returned to the wild because they were raised by humans. They wouldn't be able to survive without human help. Workers at Noah's Ark always remind visitors to the sanctuary that animals like tigers, bears, and lions don't make good pets. "Wild animals belong in the wild," says Allen.

MEET THE CREATURES			
Name	**Type of Animal**	**Weight**	**Natural Habitat**
Shere Khan	Bengal tiger	350 pounds	Asia
Baloo	American black bear	700 pounds	North America
Leo	Lion	500 pounds	Africa

Name: _____

Directions: Read the article "Furry Friends." Then answer the questions below.

1. **Which of the following sentences best states the main idea of the article?**
   A. It is against the law in Georgia to keep wild animals as pets.
   B. Tigers, bears, and lions come from different parts of the world.
   C. Tigers, bears, and lions make good pets.
   D. Surprisingly, a tiger, a bear, and a lion became good friends.

2. **What is the meaning of the word *sanctuary* as it is used in the article?**
   A. A crate where a pet animal might be kept
   B. An area where animals are protected
   C. A football field or other grassy area
   D. A person who cares for wild animals

3. **Which sentence from the article best supports the answer to question 2?**
   A. That may not sound strange. *(paragraph 1)*
   B. She works at the sanctuary, which is called Noah's Ark. *(paragraph 3)*
   C. Finally, they would have a safe place to live. *(paragraph 5)*
   D. They had not taken good care of the cubs. *(paragraph 5)*

4. **What inference about baby tigers, bears, and lions can you make from the article?**
   A. They all make good pets.
   B. They are all called cubs.
   C. They all come from Africa.
   D. They are all about the same size.

5. **Which sentence from the article best supports the answer to question 4?**
   A. But this group of animal friends was really special. *(paragraph 1)*
   B. They're also all top predators, or hunters . . . *(paragraph 2)*
   C. When the three creatures were cubs, they were found in a basement in Georgia. *(paragraph 5)*
   D. The furry pals were rescued and brought to the sanctuary. *(paragraph 5)*

6. **In paragraph 6, the author probably points out that the animals "even groomed each other" to show that they ____.**
   A. do not have any humans to care for them
   B. have a very close bond
   C. sometimes do not get along
   D. could not survive in the wild

Name: _____

7. **Which is the most likely reason that the author includes the chart "Meet the Creatures"?**

    A. To compare and contrast the three animal friends

    B. To show what each animal friend looks like

    C. To explain how people care for the three animal friends

    D. To describe how the three animal friends spend their days

8. **Why is the friendship among Shere Khan, Baloo, and Leo surprising, according to the article? Use details from the article to support your answer.**

_____

_____

_____

_____

_____

_____

_____

_____

_____

_____

Leo   Baloo   Shere Khan

Remembering Rosa

1   Imagine this: You are tired after a very long day. You get on a bus and sit near the back. Then a white man comes on the bus. The bus driver tells you to give up your seat for the man. If you don't, he'll call the police. That's what happened to Rosa Parks in 1955.

2   Back then, that's what life was like for many African Americans. Rosa Parks helped change that. Parks died in 2005. But the impact of her brave actions can still be seen today.

Taking a Stand

3   When Parks was a young woman, many states in the South had **segregation** laws. These laws separated white people and black people. Black people had to go to separate restaurants, schools, and theaters. They had to sit in the back of public buses. They also had to give up their seat if a white person wanted it.

4   Parks lived in Montgomery, Alabama. She thought these laws were wrong. She decided to do something about it. On December 1, 1955, she refused to give up her seat on a bus to a white man. Police arrested her.

Leading the Way

5   Because of what happened to Parks, black people boycotted city buses in Montgomery. Thousands refused to take the bus. They walked, carpooled, or took cabs to work for more than a year.

6   This made the rest of the nation pay attention. On November 13, 1956, the Supreme Court, our nation's highest court, made a ruling. It banned segregation on buses. Blacks can sit anywhere they want on the buses.

7   Parks inspired others to stand up for their rights too. "I just wanted to be free like everybody else," Parks once said.

Rosa Parks

Name: _____

Directions: Read the article "Remembering Rosa." Then answer the questions below.

1. What is the article "Remembering Rosa" mostly about?

    A. Why Rosa Parks had to give up her seat on a bus

    B. How Rosa Parks helped end segregation on buses

    C. Rosa Parks's childhood

    D. Why white people and black people used to go to different schools

2. Which statement best describes the author's point of view in "Remembering Rosa"?

    A. Rosa Parks was an important leader in Southern states.

    B. Rosa Parks was a creative woman who often used her imagination.

    C. Rosa Parks was a brave woman who helped shape U.S. history.

    D. Rosa Parks was a kind woman who always obeyed the law.

3. Which detail from "Remembering Rosa" best supports the answer to question 2?

    A. But the impact of her brave actions can still be seen today. *(paragraph 2)*

    B. Black people had to go to separate restaurants, schools, and theaters. *(paragraph 3)*

    C. Back then, that's what life was like for many African Americans. *(paragraph 2)*

    D. Police arrested her. *(paragraph 4)*

4. Read this sentence from paragraph 3.

> When Parks was a young woman, many states in the South had **segregation** laws.

What does the word *segregation* mean as it is used in the article?

    A. The act of giving up a bus seat

    B. The act of arresting black people

    C. Separation of black people and white people

    D. Refusal to do something that was the law

5. Which is an example of the segregation laws in parts of the South?

    A. Black people couldn't go to the same restaurants, schools, and theaters as white people.

    B. Blacks could sit anywhere they wanted on the buses.

    C. Blacks walked, carpooled, or took cabs to work for more than a year.

    D. Police arrested bus drivers who treated blacks unfairly.

Name: _____

6. Which was <u>not</u> an effect of Rosa Parks's refusal to give up her bus seat?

    A. The Supreme Court banned segregation on buses.

    B. Parks inspired others to stand up for their rights too.

    C. Black people had to sit in the back of public buses.

    D. Blacks boycotted city buses in Montgomery.

7. In paragraph 7, Rosa Parks said, "I just wanted to be free like everybody else."
   What do you think she meant by that statement? Give details to support your answer.

_____

_____

_____

_____

_____

_____

_____

Remembering Rosa

1   Imagine this: You are tired after a very long day. You get on a bus and make your way to a seat near the back. Then a white man comes on the bus. The bus driver tells you to give up your seat for the man. If you don't, he'll call the police and have you arrested. That's what happened to Rosa Parks in 1955.

2   Back then, that's how life was for many African Americans in parts of the United States. Rosa Parks helped change that. Parks died in 2005. But the impact of her brave actions can still be seen today.

Taking a Stand

3   When Parks was a young woman, many states in the South had **segregation** laws. These laws separated white people and black people. Black people had to go to separate restaurants, schools, and theaters. They had to sit in the back of public buses. They also had to give up their seat if a white person wanted it.

4   Parks lived in Montgomery, Alabama. She thought these laws were unfair. She decided to do something about it. On December 1, 1955, she refused to give up her seat on a bus to a white man. Police arrested her.

Leading the Way

5   Because of what happened to Parks, black people started to **boycott** city buses in Montgomery. Thousands refused to take the bus. Instead, they walked, carpooled, or took cabs to work for more than a year.

6   This made the rest of the nation pay attention to the unfair laws. On November 13, 1956, the Supreme Court, our nation's highest court, banned segregation on buses.

7   Parks inspired others to stand up for their rights too. "I just wanted to be free like everybody else," Parks once said.

Rosa Parks

Name: _____

Directions: Read the article "Remembering Rosa." Then answer the questions below.

1. What is the article "Remembering Rosa" mostly about?

    A. Rosa Parks's childhood

    B. Why white people and black people once went to different schools

    C. How Rosa Parks helped end segregation on buses

    D. Why Rosa Parks had to give up her seat on a bus

2. Which statement best describes the author's point of view in "Remembering Rosa"?

    A. Rosa Parks was a kind woman who always obeyed the law.

    B. Rosa Parks was a courageous woman who helped shape U.S. history.

    C. Rosa Parks was a creative woman who often used her imagination.

    D. Rosa Parks was an important leader in Southern states.

3. Which detail from "Remembering Rosa" best supports the answer to question 2?

    A. Police arrested her. *(paragraph 4)*

    B. Back then, that's how life was for many African Americans in parts of the United States. *(paragraph 2)*

    C. Black people had to go to separate restaurants, schools, and theaters. *(paragraph 3)*

    D. But the impact of her brave actions can still be seen today. *(paragraph 2)*

4. Read this sentence from paragraph 3.

    When Parks was a young woman, many states in the South had **segregation** laws.

What does the word *segregation* mean as it is used in the article?

    A. The act of arresting black people

    B. The act of giving up a bus seat

    C. Refusal to do something that was the law

    D. Separation of black people and white people

5. Which is an example of the segregation laws in parts of the South?

    A. Blacks could sit anywhere they wanted on the buses.

    B. Black people couldn't go to the same restaurants, schools, and theaters as white people.

    C. Blacks walked, carpooled, or took cabs to work for more than a year.

    D. Police arrested bus drivers who treated blacks unfairly.

Name: _____

6. Which was <u>not</u> an effect of Rosa Parks's refusal to give up her bus seat?

    A. Black people had to sit in the back of public buses.

    B. The Supreme Court banned segregation on buses.

    C. Parks inspired others to stand up for their rights too.

    D. Blacks boycotted city buses in Montgomery.

7. **Read this sentence from paragraph 5.**

    Because of what happened to Parks, black people started to **boycott** city buses in Montgomery.

    Which of the following is <u>opposite</u> to the meaning of *boycott* as it is used in this article?

    A. Refuse   **c.** Stop using

    B. Use   **D.** Reject

8. **In paragraph 7, Rosa Parks said, "I just wanted to be free like everybody else." What do you think she meant by that statement? Give details to support your answer.**

_____

_____

_____

_____

_____

_____

Remembering Rosa

1   Imagine being told to give up your seat on a bus because of your skin color. Before the 1960s, that's how life was for many African Americans in parts of the United States.

2   Rosa Parks helped change that. Parks died in 2005. But the impact of her brave actions can still be seen today.

Taking a Stand

3   During Rosa Parks's early life, many states in the South had laws that **segregated** white people and black people. Black people had to go to separate restaurants, schools, and theaters. They had to sit in the back of public buses. They also had to give up their seat if a white person wanted it.

4   Parks lived in Montgomery, Alabama. She thought these laws were unfair.

She decided to do something about it. On December 1, 1955, she refused to give up her seat on a bus to a white man. Police arrested her.

Leading the Way

5   Parks's action sparked a boycott of city buses in Montgomery. The famous African-American leader Martin Luther King Jr. helped plan the boycott. For more than a year, thousands of black people refused to take the bus. Instead, they walked, carpooled, or took cabs to work. That drew the nation's attention to the unfair laws. On November 13, 1956, the Supreme Court, our nation's highest court, banned segregation on buses.

6   Parks inspired others to stand up for their rights too. "I just wanted to be free like everybody else," Parks once said.

Rosa Parks

Name: _____

Directions: Read the article "Remembering Rosa." Then answer the questions below.

1. **What is the article "Remembering Rosa" mostly about?**

   A. Rosa Parks's childhood

   B. Why white people and black people once went to different schools

   C. Why Rosa Parks had to give up her seat on a bus

   D. How Rosa Parks helped end segregation on buses

2. **Which statement best describes the author's point of view in "Remembering Rosa"?**

   A. Rosa Parks was a courageous woman who helped shape U.S. history.

   B. Rosa Parks was a kind woman who always obeyed the law.

   C. Rosa Parks was an important leader in Southern states.

   D. Rosa Parks was a creative woman who often used her imagination.

3. **Which detail from "Remembering Rosa" best supports the answer to question 2?**

   A. Imagine being told to give up your seat on a bus because of your skin color. *(paragraph 1)*

   B. But the impact of her brave actions can still be seen today. *(paragraph 2)*

   C. Black people had to go to separate restaurants, schools, and theaters. *(paragraph 3)*

   D. Police arrested her. *(paragraph 4)*

4. **Read this sentence from paragraph 3.**

   During Rosa Parks's early life, many states in the South had laws that **segregated** white people and black people.

   What does the word *segregated* mean as it is used in the article?

   A. Made black people and white people share bus seats

   B. Separated black people and white people

   C. Arrested black people

   D. Gave black people and white people the same rights

5. **Which is an example of the segregation laws in parts of the South?**

   A. Blacks could sit anywhere they wanted on the buses.

   B. Blacks walked, carpooled, or took cabs to work for more than a year.

   C. Police arrested bus drivers who treated blacks unfairly.

   D. Black people couldn't go to the same restaurants, schools, and theaters as white people.

Name: _____

6. Which was <u>not</u> an effect of Rosa Parks's refusal to give up her bus seat?

   A. Black people had to sit in the back of public buses.

   B. Blacks boycotted city buses in Montgomery.

   C. The Supreme Court banned segregation on buses.

   D. Parks inspired others to stand up for their rights too.

7. Read this sentence from paragraph 5.

    Parks's action sparked a **boycott** of city buses in Montgomery.

   Which of the following is <u>opposite</u> to the meaning of *boycott* as it is used in this article?

   A. Use   **C.** Refusal

   B. Disuse   **D.** Rejection

8. In paragraph 7, Rosa Parks said, "I just wanted to be free like everybody else."
What do you think she meant by that statement? Give details to support your answer.

_____

_____

_____

_____

_____

_____

Ferrets Make a Comeback

1   Scientist Dean Biggins studies black-footed ferrets. But he hardly sees these animals in the wild. They are very rare.

2   Millions of black-footed ferrets used to live across North America's prairie. But about 40 years ago, scientists thought the ferrets had all died out. They were wrong. Now scientists like Biggins are helping the animals make a comeback.

Disappearing Food

3   Black-footed ferrets mainly eat prairie dogs. A prairie dog is a type of squirrel that lives underground. After eating a prairie dog, a ferret moves into its home.

4   In the 1900s, ranchers killed millions of prairie dogs. The prairie dogs were eating the grass their cattle needed for food. Fewer prairie dogs meant less food for the ferrets. They had a hard time finding shelter too. As a result, the number of ferrets dropped.

Back From the Dead

5   By 1979, scientists couldn't find any ferrets. They thought the ferrets had all died out. But two years later, an amazing thing happened. A dog found a dead black-footed ferret near a town in Wyoming.

6   Scientists rushed to the town. There they found a small group of ferrets. There were prairie dogs in the area too. But both species faced a big problem. A disease was killing them. By the late 1980s, only 18 ferrets remained.

To the Rescue

7   To save the ferrets, scientists took them to a special center. There they helped the animals breed. They gave them medicine to protect them from the disease. They also taught the ferrets skills to help them survive in the wild.

8   Today, about 500 ferrets live in the wild. But the animals are still in danger. Biggins says it's important to protect them before it's too late.

9   "We should not be waiting so long to take action," says Biggins. "And we certainly should be thinking ahead."

A black-footed ferret in the wild

Name: _____

Directions: Read the article "Ferrets Make a Comeback."
Then answer the questions below.

1. **What is the main idea of the article?**

   A. Scientist Dean Biggins realized ferrets had not all died out.

   B. Black-footed ferrets mainly eat prairie dogs.

   C. In the 1900s, ranchers killed millions of prairie dogs.

   D. Black-footed ferrets almost died out, but scientists are helping them
   make a comeback.

2. **According to the article, why did ranchers kill prairie dogs?**

   A. They wanted to make sure their cattle had enough grass to eat.

   B. They mistook them for black-footed ferrets.

   C. They didn't want to catch diseases from them.

   D. They wanted to protect black-footed ferrets from them.

3. **Which best describes the purpose of the section "Disappearing Food"?**

   A. To compare black-footed ferrets and prairie dogs

   B. To describe how scientists are protecting black-footed ferrets

   C. To explain what happened to black-footed ferrets when prairie dogs were killed

   D. To suggest a solution to the problem of ranchers killing prairie dogs

4. **According to the article, which of the following statements is true about the town
   in Wyoming?**

   A. A small group of black-footed ferrets was found in the area.

   B. A disease was killing the people who live in the town.

   C. There were no prairie dogs in the area.

   D. A medical center in town was treating black-footed ferrets.

5. **According to the article, what are scientists <u>not</u> doing to help black-footed ferrets
   make a comeback?**

   A. Giving ferrets medicine

   B. Using dogs to find surviving ferrets

   C. Helping ferrets breed

   D. Teaching ferrets how to survive in the wild

6. Which statement is supported by the article?

A. Breeding black-footed ferrets in special centers has harmed the animals.

B. Prairie dogs must survive in order for black-footed ferrets to survive.

C. Today, black-footed ferrets live only in special animal centers.

D. Black-footed ferrets will likely die out in a few years.

7. Which detail from the article best shows that black-footed ferrets are in danger?

A. A dog found a dead black-footed ferret near a town in Wyoming. *(paragraph 5)*

B. Black-footed ferrets mainly eat prairie dogs. *(paragraph 3)*

C. Millions of black-footed ferrets used to live across North America's prairie. *(paragraph 2)*

D. Biggins says it's important to protect them before it's too late. *(paragraph 8)*

8. Humans have affected black-footed ferrets in many ways. Based on the article, how have humans harmed the ferrets? How have humans helped them? Use at least one detail from the text in your answer.

_____

_____

_____

_____

_____

_____

Ferrets Make a Comeback

1   Scientist Dean Biggins studies black-footed ferrets. But he hardly sees these animals in the wild. They are very rare.

2   Millions of black-footed ferrets used to live across North America's prairie. But about 40 years ago, scientists thought the ferrets had all died out. They were wrong. Now scientists like Biggins are helping the animals make a comeback.

Disappearing Food

3   Black-footed ferrets mainly hunt prairie dogs. A prairie dog is a type of squirrel that lives underground. After eating a prairie dog, a ferret moves into its home.

4   In the 1900s, ranchers killed millions of prairie dogs. The prairie dogs were eating the grass their cattle needed for food. Fewer prairie dogs meant less food for the ferrets. They had a hard time finding shelter too. As a result, the number of ferrets dropped.

Back From the Dead

5   By 1979, scientists couldn't find any ferrets. They thought the ferrets had all died out. But two years later, an amazing thing happened. A dog found a dead black-footed ferret near the town of Meeteetse, Wyoming.

6   Scientists rushed to the area. There they found a small group of ferrets. They found prairie dogs nearby too. But both species had a big problem. A disease was killing them. By the late 1980s, only 18 ferrets remained.

To the Rescue

7   To save the ferrets, scientists took them to a special center. There they helped the animals breed. They gave them medicine to protect them from the disease. They also taught the ferrets skills to help them survive in the wild.

8   Today, about 500 ferrets live in the wild. But the animals are still **endangered**. Biggins says it's important to protect them before it's too late.

9   "We should not be waiting so long to take action," says Biggins. "And we certainly should be thinking ahead."

A black-footed ferret in the wild

Name: _____

Directions: Read the article "Ferrets Make a Comeback."
Then answer the questions below.

1. What is the main idea of the article?

A. Black-footed ferrets almost died out, but scientists are helping them make a comeback.

B. Black-footed ferrets live on the prairie and rely on prairie dogs for their survival.

C. Scientist Dean Biggins realized ferrets had not all died out when a dog found a dead ferret near Meeteetse, Wyoming.

D. In the 1900s, ranchers killed millions of prairie dogs.

2. According to the article, why did ranchers kill prairie dogs?

A. They mistook them for black-footed ferrets.

B. They wanted to make sure their cattle had enough grass to eat.

C. They didn't want to catch diseases from them.

D. They wanted to protect black-footed ferrets from them.

3. Which best describes the purpose of the section "Disappearing Food"?

A. To compare black-footed ferrets and prairie dogs

B. To explain what happened to black-footed ferrets when prairie dogs were killed

C. To suggest a solution to the problem of ranchers killing prairie dogs

D. To describe the steps scientists took to protect black-footed ferrets

4. According to the article, which of the following statements is true about the town of Meeteetse, Wyoming?

A. There were no prairie dogs in the area.

B. A disease was killing the people who live in the town.

C. A small group of black-footed ferrets was found in the area.

D. A medical center in town was treating black-footed ferrets.

5. According to the article, scientists are helping black-footed ferrets make a comeback in all of the following ways except ____.

A. Helping ferrets breed

B. Teaching ferrets survival skills

C. Using dogs to find surviving ferrets

D. Giving ferrets medicine

6. Which statement is supported by the article?

   A. Today, black-footed ferrets live only in special animal centers.

   B. Breeding black-footed ferrets in special centers has harmed the animals.

   C. Black-footed ferrets will likely die out in a few years.

   D. The survival of black-footed ferrets depends on the survival of prairie dogs.

7. What does the word *endangered* mean as it is used in paragraph 8?

   A. Dangerous

   B. Killed off completely

   C. At risk of dying out

   D. Easy to find

8. Which detail from the article best shows that black-footed ferrets are endangered?

   A. Biggins says it's important to protect them before it's too late. *(paragraph 8)*

   B. Millions of black-footed ferrets used to live across North America's prairie. *(paragraph 2)*

   C. Black-footed ferrets mainly hunt prairie dogs. *(paragraph 3)*

   D. A dog found a dead black-footed ferret near the town of Meeteetse, Wyoming. *(paragraph 5)*

9. Humans have affected black-footed ferrets in many ways. Based on the article, how have humans harmed the ferrets? How have humans helped them? Use at least two details from the text in your answer.

_____

_____

_____

_____

_____

Ferrets Make a Comeback

1   Scientist Dean Biggins studies black-footed ferrets. But he seldom spots the animals in the wild. They are one of the rarest animals in the world.

2   Millions of black-footed ferrets once lived across North America's prairie. But about 40 years ago, scientists thought the ferrets had all died out. They were wrong. Now scientists like Biggins are helping the animals make a comeback.

Disappearing Food

3   Black-footed ferrets mainly hunt prairie dogs. A prairie dog is a type of squirrel that lives underground. After eating a prairie dog, a ferret moves into its home.

4   In the 1900s, ranchers killed millions of prairie dogs. The prairie dogs were eating the grass their cattle needed for food. With fewer prairie dogs around, the ferrets had a hard time finding both food and shelter. As a result, the number of ferrets dropped too.

Back From the Dead

5   By 1979, scientists couldn't find any ferrets. They thought the ferrets had died out. But two years later, an amazing thing happened. A dog found a dead black-footed ferret near the town of Meeteetse, Wyoming.

6   Scientists rushed to the area and found a small group of ferrets that had survived. There were prairie dogs in the area too. But both species were facing a big problem. A disease called sylvatic plague was killing them. By the late 1980s, just 18 ferrets remained.

To the Rescue

7   To save the ferrets, scientists took them to a special center. There they helped the animals breed and gave them medicine. They also taught the ferrets skills to help them survive in the wild.

8   Today, about 500 ferrets live in the wild. But the animals are still **endangered**. Biggins says it's important to protect them before it's too late.

9   "We should not be waiting so long to take action, and we certainly should be thinking ahead," says Biggins.

A black-footed ferret in the wild

Name: _____

Directions: Read the article "Ferrets Make a Comeback."
Then answer the questions below.

1. **What is the main idea of the article?**
   A. In the 1900s, ranchers killed millions of prairie dogs.
   B. Black-footed ferrets live on the prairie and rely on prairie dogs for their survival.
   C. Black-footed ferrets almost died out, but scientists are helping them make a comeback.
   D. Scientist Dean Biggins realized ferrets had not all died out when a dog found a dead ferret near Meeteetse, Wyoming.

2. **According to the article, why did ranchers kill prairie dogs?**
   A. They mistook them for black-footed ferrets.
   B. They didn't want to catch diseases from them.
   C. They wanted to make sure their cattle had enough grass to eat.
   D. They wanted to protect black-footed ferrets from them.

3. **Which best describes the purpose of the section "Disappearing Food"?**
   A. To compare black-footed ferrets and prairie dogs
   B. To describe the steps scientists took to protect black-footed ferrets
   C. To suggest a solution to the problem of ranchers killing prairie dogs
   D. To explain what happened to black-footed ferrets when prairie dogs were killed

4. **Which of the following statements about sylvatic plague is true?**
   A. It affects only black-footed ferrets.
   B. It is the main reason so many black-footed ferrets died in the early 1900s.
   C. It affected the small population of black-footed ferrets discovered in the 1980s.
   D. It cannot be treated with medicine.

5. **According to the article, scientists are helping black-footed ferrets make a comeback in all of the following ways except ___.**
   A. using dogs to find surviving ferrets
   B. helping ferrets breed
   C. teaching ferrets survival skills
   D. giving ferrets medicine

6. Which statement is supported by the article?

　A. Breeding black-footed ferrets in special centers has harmed the animals.

　B. The survival of black-footed ferrets depends on the survival of prairie dogs.

　C. Today, black-footed ferrets live only in special animal centers.

　D. Black-footed ferrets will likely die out in a few years.

7. What does the word *endangered* mean as it is used in paragraph 8?

　A. Killed off completely

　B. At risk of dying out

　C. Easy to find

　D. Dangerous

8. Which detail from the article best shows that black-footed ferrets are endangered?

　A. Millions of black-footed ferrets once lived across North America's prairie. *(paragraph 2)*

　B. Black-footed ferrets mainly hunt prairie dogs. *(paragraph 3)*

　C. A dog found a dead black-footed ferret near the town of Meeteetse, Wyoming. *(paragraph 5)*

　D. Biggins says it's important to protect them before it's too late. *(paragraph 8)*

9. Humans have affected black-footed ferrets in many ways. Based on the article, how have humans harmed the ferrets? How have humans helped them? Use at least two details from the text in your answer.

_____

_____

_____

_____

_____

Connecting the World

1   Do you go online to look up information? Maybe watch videos or chat with friends? In many places, kids can't get online. More than half of the people in the world can't connect to the internet. The technology company Google wants to change that.

No Connection

2   Most people in the United States can get on the internet. They can get online at home, at the library, or on their cell phones. But in some parts of the world, people have to walk for miles just to get online. Why? To get internet service, you need a lot of equipment. You need long, underground cables to connect buildings to the internet. The cables carry information back and forth. But it costs too much to get cables to faraway places.

3   Getting online can change people's lives. A village in the African country of Zambia recently got an internet connection. This helped farmers there to learn about new crops. They could order seeds online. Doctors could read about new ways to treat people. Villagers could look for new jobs.

High in the Sky

4   Having an internet connection helps people. So Google made giant balloons to carry wireless internet equipment. They filled the balloons with helium. That's the same gas that makes party balloons float. The balloons rise more than 12 miles above the Earth. That's almost twice as high as airplanes fly! Antennas on the balloons send information to and from antennas on people's houses.

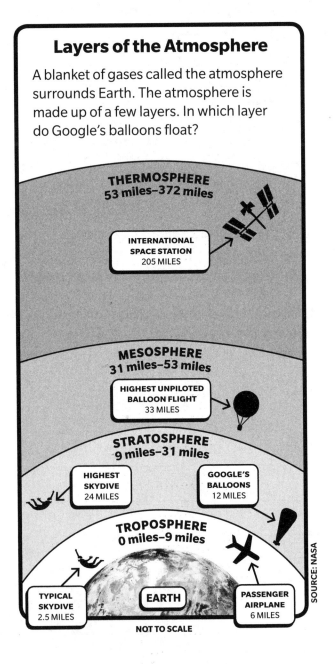

Layers of the Atmosphere

A blanket of gases called the atmosphere surrounds Earth. The atmosphere is made up of a few layers. In which layer do Google's balloons float?

THERMOSPHERE
53 miles–372 miles

INTERNATIONAL SPACE STATION
205 MILES

MESOSPHERE
31 miles–53 miles

HIGHEST UNPILOTED BALLOON FLIGHT
33 MILES

STRATOSPHERE
9 miles–31 miles

HIGHEST SKYDIVE
24 MILES

GOOGLE'S BALLOONS
12 MILES

TROPOSPHERE
0 miles–9 miles

TYPICAL SKYDIVE
2.5 MILES

EARTH

PASSENGER AIRPLANE
6 MILES

NOT TO SCALE

SOURCE: NASA

One of Google's internet-providing balloons

Put to the Test

5   In June 2013, Google tested the balloons in New Zealand. Workers attached antennas to 50 houses there. Then they launched 30 balloons.

6   The balloons floated across the sky. Some of them traveled above Charles Nimmo's farm. Charles got on his computer. The antenna on his house sent a signal to the antennas on the balloons. Then he tried to connect. "It worked!" says Charles. "I even loaded a video."

Up, Up, and Away

7   Since then, Google has launched hundreds of balloons into the air. The technology has come a long way. In 2013, the balloons could stay in the air for about five days. Now they last about 100 days.

8   "We're getting close to the point where we can bring the internet to people around the world," says project leader Mike Cassidy.

Name: _____

Directions: Read the article "Connecting the World."
Then answer the questions below.

1. **What is the main problem described in the article?**

   A. Google's giant balloons are in the way of airplanes.

   B. Google doesn't have enough balloons to provide internet access
      to everyone in the world.

   C. Everyone in the world has internet service.

   D. Many people in the world can't get online.

2. **Which detail best supports the answer to question 1?**

   A. The balloons rise more than 12 miles above the Earth. *(paragraph 4)*

   B. Most people in the United States can get on the internet. *(paragraph 2)*

   C. More than half of the people in the world can't connect to the internet. *(paragraph 1)*

   D. Since then, Google has launched hundreds of balloons into the air. *(paragraph 7)*

3. **In paragraph 3, the author writes about a village that recently got an internet
   connection. What is the most likely reason the author includes this paragraph?**

   A. To show how getting online helped the people in that village

   B. To point out how far away the village is from the United States

   C. To tell where a Google balloon was first tested

   D. To describe the lives of various people in the village

4. **Which question can be answered by reading the section "High in the Sky"?**

   A. How can getting online change people's lives?

   B. Why is it difficult to connect to the internet in some parts of the world?

   C. When did Google test the balloon project for the first time?

   D. How do Google's balloons float in the air?

5. **Which detail from the section "High in the Sky" best supports the answer
   to question 4?**

   A. They filled the balloons with helium.

   B. Having an internet connection helps people.

   C. So Google made giant balloons to carry wireless internet equipment.

   D. Antennas on the balloons send information to and from antennas on
      people's houses.

Name: _____

6. How do Google's balloons help people connect to the internet?

   A. They carry long cables.

   B. They carry computers and cell phones.

   C. They carry wireless internet equipment.

   D. They carry people to schools and libraries.

7. Which section of the article would be most helpful for finding facts about the first time Google tested the balloons?

   A. "No Connection"

   B. "High in the Sky"

   C. "Put to the Test"

   D. "Up, Up, and Away"

8. What does the diagram help you understand?

   A. What Google's balloons look like from the ground

   B. How high Google's balloons can fly

   C. How big Google's balloons are

   D. What makes Google's balloons float

9. Read the sentences below from paragraph 7.

   In 2013, the balloons could stay in the air for about five days. Now they last about 100 days.

   Which best describes the relationship between the sentences?

   A. The sentences describe similarities between two types of balloons.

   B. The sentences list steps for how Google makes its balloons.

   C. The sentences explain how Google's balloons stay in the air for a long time.

   D. The sentences show how Google's balloons have changed over time.

10. Based on the article, why do you think Google wants to bring the internet to more people around the world? Use details from the article to support your answer.

_____

_____

_____

_____

_____

Connecting the World

1   Do you use a computer? If so, you might go online to look up information, watch videos, or chat with friends. But in many places, kids can't get online. More than half of the people in the world don't have internet access.

2   The technology company Google is hoping to change that. It wants to send special balloons high up into the air. These balloons can help a lot more people get online.

No Connection

3   Most people in the United States can connect to the internet. They can get online at home, at the library, or on their cell phones. But in some parts of the world, people have to walk to a location miles away to get online.

4   Why is it so hard to get online in these places? Most internet service requires a lot of equipment. Buildings are often connected to the internet through long underground cables. These cables carry information back and forth. But in **remote** places, it's too expensive to connect everyone this way. Cables would need to stretch across very long distances to reach these faraway spots.

5   But getting online can change people's lives. Elizabeth Belding would agree with that. She's a computer scientist at the University of California, Santa Barbara. She recently studied a village in the African country of Zambia that had just gotten an internet connection. Going online allowed farmers there to learn about new crops and order seeds. Doctors could read about new ways to treat people. Villagers could find new jobs.

High in the Sky

6   Having online access can benefit everyone. Google wants to bring the internet to more people around the world. So people at the company came up with

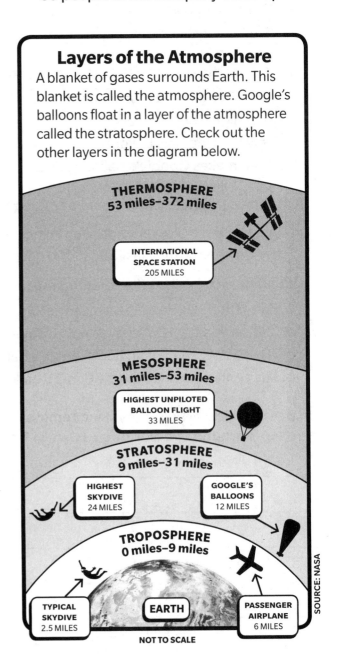

Layers of the Atmosphere

A blanket of gases surrounds Earth. This blanket is called the atmosphere. Google's balloons float in a layer of the atmosphere called the stratosphere. Check out the other layers in the diagram below.

THERMOSPHERE
53 miles–372 miles

INTERNATIONAL SPACE STATION
205 MILES

MESOSPHERE
31 miles–53 miles

HIGHEST UNPILOTED BALLOON FLIGHT
33 MILES

STRATOSPHERE
9 miles–31 miles

HIGHEST SKYDIVE
24 MILES

GOOGLE'S BALLOONS
12 MILES

TROPOSPHERE
0 miles–9 miles

TYPICAL SKYDIVE
2.5 MILES

EARTH

PASSENGER AIRPLANE
6 MILES

NOT TO SCALE

SOURCE: NASA

One of Google's internet-providing balloons

the idea of using giant balloons to carry wireless internet equipment.

7   The balloons are filled with helium. That's the same gas that makes party balloons float. The helium lifts the balloons more than 12 miles above Earth's surface. That's almost twice as high as passenger airplanes fly! People on the ground move the balloons using remote controllers. Antennas aboard the balloons beam information to and from antennas on people's houses.

Put to the Test

8   In June 2013, Google tested the balloons for the first time. Workers attached antennas to 50 houses in New Zealand, an island country in the Pacific Ocean. Then they launched 30 balloons.

9   The balloons drifted through the sky. Some of them traveled above Charles Nimmo's farm. Charles got on his computer. The antenna on his house sent a signal to the antennas on the balloons. Then he tried to connect.

10   "It worked!" says Charles. "I even loaded a video."

Up, Up, and Away

11   Since its first test, Google has launched hundreds of balloons into the air. The technology has come a long way. In 2013, the balloons could stay in the air for about five days. Now they last about 100 days.

12   "We're getting close to the point where we can bring the internet to people around the world," says project leader Mike Cassidy.

Name: _____

Directions: Read the article "Connecting the World."
Then answer the questions below.

1. What is the main problem described in the article?

    A. Google doesn't have enough balloons to provide internet access to everyone in the world.

    B. Everyone in the world has internet service.

    C. Many people in the world can't get online.

    D. Google's giant balloons are in the way of passenger airplanes.

2. Which detail best supports the answer to question 1?

    A. More than half of the people in the world don't have internet access. *(paragraph 1)*

    B. Since its first test, Google has launched hundreds of balloons into the air. *(paragraph 11)*

    C. If so, you might go online to look up information, watch videos, or chat with friends. *(paragraph 1)*

    D. The helium lifts the balloons more than 12 miles above Earth's surface. *(paragraph 7)*

3. In paragraph 4, the author uses the word *remote*. Which of the following phrases from paragraph 4 helps the reader understand what *remote* means?

    A. Requires a lot of equipment

    B. These faraway spots

    C. Connected to the internet

    D. Too expensive

4. Which question can be answered by reading the section "High in the Sky"?

    A. How do Google's balloons float in the air?

    B. How can getting online change people's lives?

    C. When did Google test the balloon project for the first time?

    D. Why is it difficult to connect to the internet in some parts of the world?

5. Which detail from the section "High in the Sky" best supports the answer to question 4?

    A. Google wants to bring the internet to more people around the world.

    B. The balloons are filled with helium.

    C. So people at the company came up with the idea of using giant balloons to carry wireless internet equipment.

    D. Antennas aboard the balloons beam information to and from antennas on people's houses.

Name: _____

6. **How do Google's balloons help people connect to the internet?**

   A. They carry wireless internet equipment.

   B. They carry long cables.

   C. They carry computers and cell phones.

   D. They carry people to schools and libraries.

7. **Which section of the article would be most helpful for finding facts about the first time Google tested the balloons?**

   A. "No Connection"

   B. "High in the Sky"

   C. "Put to the Test"

   D. "Up, Up, and Away"

8. **What does the diagram help you understand?**

   A. What Google's balloons look like from the ground

   B. How big Google's balloons are

   C. What makes Google's balloons float

   D. How high Google's balloons can fly

9. **Read the sentences below from paragraph 11.**

   In 2013, the balloons could stay in the air for about five days. Now they last about 100 days.

   Which best describes the relationship between the sentences?

   A. The sentences show how Google's balloons have changed over time.

   B. The sentences describe similarities between two types of balloons.

   C. The sentences list steps for how Google makes its balloons.

   D. The sentences explain how Google's balloons stay in the air for a long time.

10. **Based on the article, why do you think Google wants to bring the internet to more people around the world? Use details from the article to support your answer.**

_____

_____

_____

_____

_____

Connecting the World

1   Do you use a computer? If so, you might go online to look up information, watch videos, or chat with friends. But in many places, kids can't get online. More than half of the people in the world don't have internet access.

2   The technology company Google is hoping to change that. It wants to send special balloons high up into the air to help a lot more people get online.

No Connection

3   Most people in the United States can get on the internet at home, at the library, or on their cell phones. But in some parts of the world, people have to walk to a location miles away to get online.

4   Why is it so hard to get online in these places? Most internet service requires a lot of equipment. Buildings are often connected to the internet through long underground cables that carry information back and forth. But in **remote** places, it's too expensive to connect everyone this way. Cables would need to stretch across very long distances to reach these faraway spots.

5   But getting online can change people's lives. Elizabeth Belding would agree with that. She's a computer scientist at the University of California, Santa Barbara. Belding recently studied a village in the African country of Zambia that had just gotten an internet connection. Going online allowed farmers there to learn about new crops and order seeds. Doctors could read about new ways to treat people. Villagers could find new jobs.

High in the Sky

6   Because of all the benefits of online access, Google wants to bring the internet to more people around the world. So people at the company came up with

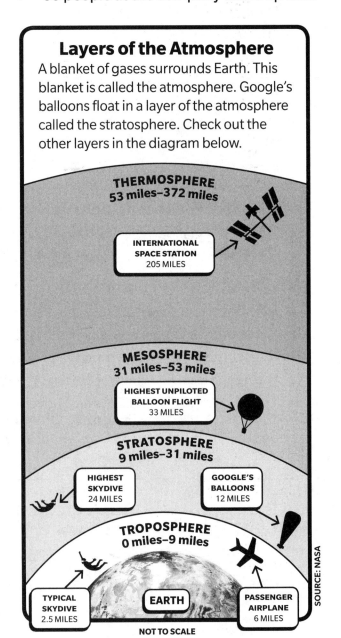

Layers of the Atmosphere

A blanket of gases surrounds Earth. This blanket is called the atmosphere. Google's balloons float in a layer of the atmosphere called the stratosphere. Check out the other layers in the diagram below.

THERMOSPHERE
53 miles–372 miles

INTERNATIONAL SPACE STATION
205 MILES

MESOSPHERE
31 miles–53 miles

HIGHEST UNPILOTED BALLOON FLIGHT
33 MILES

STRATOSPHERE
9 miles–31 miles

HIGHEST SKYDIVE
24 MILES

GOOGLE'S BALLOONS
12 MILES

TROPOSPHERE
0 miles–9 miles

TYPICAL SKYDIVE
2.5 MILES

EARTH

PASSENGER AIRPLANE
6 MILES

NOT TO SCALE

SOURCE: NASA

One of Google's internet-providing balloons

the idea of using giant balloons to carry wireless internet equipment.

7   The balloons are filled with helium, the same gas that makes party balloons float. The helium lifts the balloons more than 12 miles above Earth's surface. That's almost twice as high as passenger airplanes fly! People on the ground move the balloons using remote controllers. Antennas aboard the balloons beam information to and from antennas on people's houses.

Put to the Test

8   In June 2013, Google tested the balloons for the first time. Workers attached antennas to 50 houses in New Zealand, an island country in the Pacific Ocean. Then they launched 30 balloons.

9   The balloons drifted through the sky. Some of them traveled above Charles Nimmo's farm. Charles got on his computer. The antenna on his house sent a signal to the antennas on the balloons. Then he tried to connect.

10   "It worked!" says Charles. "I even loaded a video."

Up, Up, and Away

11   Since its first test, Google has launched hundreds of balloons into the air. The technology has come a long way. In 2013, the balloons could stay in the air for about five days. Now they last about 100 days.

12   "We're getting close to the point where we can bring the internet to people around the world," says project leader Mike Cassidy.

Directions: Read the article "Connecting the World."
Then answer the questions below.

1. **What is the main problem described in the article?**

   A. Everyone in the world has internet service.

   B. Many people in the world can't get online.

   C. Google's giant balloons are in the way of passenger airplanes.

   D. Google doesn't have enough balloons to provide internet access to everyone in the world.

2. **Which detail best supports the answer to question 1?**

   A. If so, you might go online to look up information, watch videos, or chat with friends. *(paragraph 1)*

   B. More than half of the people in the world don't have internet access. *(paragraph 1)*

   C. The helium lifts the balloons more than 12 miles above Earth's surface. *(paragraph 7)*

   D. Since its first test, Google has launched hundreds of balloons into the air. *(paragraph 11)*

3. **In paragraph 4, the author uses the word** *remote*. **Which of the following phrases from paragraph 4 helps the reader understand what** *remote* **means?**

   A. Requires a lot of equipment

   B. Connected to the internet

   C. Too expensive

   D. These faraway spots

4. **Which question can be answered by reading the section "High in the Sky"?**

   A. Why is it difficult to connect to the internet in some parts of the world?

   B. How can getting online change people's lives?

   C. How do Google's balloons float in the air?

   D. When did Google test the balloon project for the first time?

5. **Which detail from the section "High in the Sky" best supports the answer to question 4?**

   A. . . . Google wants to bring the internet to more people around the world.

   B. So people at the company came up with the idea of using giant balloons to carry wireless internet equipment.

   C. Antennas aboard the balloons beam information to and from antennas on people's houses.

   D. The balloons are filled with helium, the same gas that makes party balloons float.

6. How do Google's balloons help people connect to the internet?

    A. They carry long cables.

    B. They carry wireless internet equipment.

    C. They carry computers and cell phones.

    D. They carry people to schools and libraries.

7. Which section of the article would be most helpful for finding facts about the first time Google tested the balloons?

    A. "No Connection"

    B. "High in the Sky"

    C. "Put to the Test"

    D. "Up, Up, and Away"

8. What does the diagram help you understand?

    A. How high Google's balloons can fly

    B. How big Google's balloons are

    C. What makes Google's balloons float

    D. What Google's balloons look like from the ground

9. Read the sentences below from paragraph 11.

    In 2013, the balloons could stay in the air for about five days. Now they last about 100 days.

    Which best describes the relationship between the sentences?

    A. The sentences describe similarities between two types of balloons.

    B. The sentences show how Google's balloons have changed over time.

    C. The sentences list steps for how Google makes its balloons.

    D. The sentences explain how Google's balloons stay in the air for a long time.

10. Based on the article, why do you think Google wants to bring the internet to more people around the world? Use details from the article to support your answer.

_____

_____

_____

_____

_____

Answer Key

THEY'RE BACK

page 7
1. a **2.** c **3.** a **4.** b **5.** Answers will vary.
Sample response: *The trees in Brazil were being cut down. The conservation groups bought land so the trees there wouldn't be cut down. Because the macaws had a place to live, they were able to make a comeback.*

page 9
1. d **2.** b **3.** c **4.** a **5.** Answers will vary.
Sample response: *The trees in Brazil were being cut down. The conservation groups bought land so the trees there wouldn't be cut down. Because the macaws had a place to live, they were able to make a comeback.*

page 11
1. b **2.** a **3.** a **4.** b **5.** Answers will vary.
Sample response: *The trees in Brazil were being cut down. The conservation groups bought land so that the trees there wouldn't be cut down. Because the macaws had a place to live, they were able to make a comeback.*

TEACHING MACHINES

page 13
1. c **2.** a **3.** d **4.** a **5.** Answers will vary.
Sample response: *The robot language teachers and Saya are machines used in classrooms. They help teach students. Robot language teachers are used in South Korea. They mainly teach English. Saya is used in Japan. It does many tasks, such as take attendance and tell noisy kids to be quiet.*

page 15
1. d **2.** b **3.** b **4.** d **5.** Answers will vary.
Sample response: *The robot language teachers and Saya are machines that are used in classrooms to help teach students. Robot language teachers are used in South Korea. They mainly teach English. Saya is used in Japan, and it does many tasks, such as take attendance and tell noisy kids to be quiet.*

page 17
1. b **2.** d **3.** a **4.** b **5.** Answers will vary.
Sample response: *The robot language teachers and Saya are machines that are used in classrooms to help teach students. Robot language teachers are used in South Korea and mainly teach English. Saya is used in Japan and does many tasks, such as take attendance and tell noisy kids to be quiet.*

SEAL RESCUE

page 19
1. c **2.** b **3.** a **4.** b **5.** Answers will vary.
Sample response: *Way humans can hurt seals: Crowd around a seal pup OR leave garbage, like plastic bags, on the beach. Way humans can help seals: Make sure seals aren't disturbed OR keep the beach clean.*

page 21
1. a **2.** c **3.** d **4.** d **5.** Answers will vary.
Sample response: *Ways humans can hurt seals: Crowd around a seal pup and leave garbage, like plastic bags, on the beach. Ways humans can help seals: Make sure seals aren't disturbed and keep the beach clean.*

page 23
1. d **2.** d **3.** c **4.** a **5.** Answers will vary.
Sample response: *Ways humans can hurt seals: Crowd around a seal pup and leave garbage, like plastic bags, on the beach. Ways humans can help seals: Make sure seals aren't disturbed and keep the beach clean.*

I SURVIVED A TORNADO

page 25
1. b **2.** c **3.** Answers will vary. Sample response: *The tornado destroyed parts of their house. For example, their whole living room, garage, and part of the kitchen were gone.*
4. Answers will vary. Sample response: *The map shows where Tornado Alley is in the United States. The article did not include this information.*

page 27
1. a **2.** b **3.** Answers will vary. Sample response: *The tornado destroyed parts of their house. For example, their whole living room, garage, and part of the kitchen were gone. They had to move to a new house.* **4.** Answers will vary. Sample response: *The map shows where Tornado Alley is in the United States. It also shows where Logan's town, Phil Campbell, is located. The article did not include this information.*

page 29
1. c **2.** d **3.** Answers will vary. Sample response: *The tornado destroyed parts of their house. For example, their whole living room, garage, and part of the kitchen were gone. They had to move to a new house.* **4.** Answers will vary. Sample response: *The map shows where Tornado Alley is in the United States. It also shows where Logan's town, Phil Campbell, is located. The article did not include this information.*

TRACKING TURTLES

page 31
1. b **2.** b **3.** c **4.** c **5.** a **6.** d **7.** b **8.** a

page 34
1. c **2.** c **3.** d **4.** a **5.** b **6.** b **7.** c **8.** Answers will vary. Sample response: *Scientists think baby turtles go to the center of the currents because there are large seaweed patches there. Seaweed patches are good places for baby turtles to grow. For example, the article says that the turtles can float on the seaweed to hide from sharks. They can also stay warm there. The seaweed patches are also good places for the baby sea turtles to find plenty of insects and other food to eat.*

page 37
1. d **2.** d **3.** b **4.** b **5.** d **6.** a **7.** c **8.** Answers will vary. Sample response: *Scientists think baby turtles go to the center of the currents because there are large seaweed patches there. Seaweed patches are good places for baby turtles to grow. For example, the article says that the turtles can float on the seaweed to hide from sharks. They can also stay warm there. The seaweed patches are also good places for the baby sea turtles to find plenty of insects and other food to eat.*

FURRY FRIENDS

page 40
1. b **2.** c **3.** a **4.** b **5.** a **6.** d **7.** Answers will vary. Sample response: *The friendship among Shere Khan, Baloo, and Leo is surprising for two reasons. For one thing, the three animals would never have come face to face in the wild. The article states that "each animal came from a different part of the world." Bengal tigers like Shere Khan come from Asia, black bears like Baloo come from North America, and lions like Leo come from Africa. In addition, the three creatures are all top hunters. According to a worker at the sanctuary, they probably would have fought each other for food if they ever did meet in the wild.*

page 43
1. c **2.** a **3.** b **4.** c **5.** d **6.** a **7.** d **8.** Answers will vary. Sample response: *The friendship among Shere Khan, Baloo, and Leo is surprising for two reasons. For one thing, the three animals would never have come face to face in the wild. The article states that "they each came from different parts of the world." Bengal tigers like Shere Khan come from Asia, black bears like Baloo come from North America, and lions like Leo come from Africa. In addition, the three creatures are all top predators. According to a worker at the sanctuary, they probably would have fought each other for food if they ever did meet in the wild.*

page 46
1. d **2.** b **3.** c **4.** b **5.** c **6.** b **7.** a **8.** Answers will vary. Sample response: *The friendship among Shere Khan, Baloo, and Leo is surprising for two reasons. For one thing, the three animals would never have come face to face in the wild. The article states that "the three species came from different parts of the world." Bengal tigers like Shere Khan come from Asia, black bears like Baloo come from North America, and lions like Leo come from Africa. In addition, the three creatures are all top predators. According to a worker at the sanctuary, they probably would have fought each other for food if they ever did meet in the wild.*

REMEMBERING ROSA

page 49
1. b **2.** c **3.** a **4.** c **5.** a **6.** c **7.** Answers will vary. Sample response: *Rosa Parks meant that she wanted to have the same rights as white people. She wanted to be able to sit anywhere on the bus, not just in the back. She didn't want to have to give up her seat to a white person. She wanted to be able to go to the same restaurants, schools, or theaters as white people. She wanted to be treated fairly.*

page 52
1. c **2.** b **3.** d **4.** d **5.** b **6.** a **7.** b
8. Answers will vary. Sample response: *Rosa Parks meant she wanted to have the same rights as white people. She wanted to be able to sit anywhere on the bus, not just in the back, and she didn't want to have to give up her seat to a white person. She wanted to be able to go to the same restaurants, schools, or theaters as white people. In other words, she wanted to be treated fairly.*

page 55
1. d **2.** a **3.** b **4.** b **5.** d **6.** b **7.** a
8. Answers will vary. Sample response: *Rosa Parks meant she wanted to have the same rights as white people. She wanted to be able to sit anywhere on the bus, not just in the back, and she didn't want to have to give up her seat to a white person. She wanted to be able to go to the same restaurants, schools, or theaters as white people. In other words, she wanted to be treated fairly.*

FERRETS MAKE A COMEBACK

page 58
1. d **2.** a **3.** c **4.** a **5.** b **6.** b **7.** d
8. Answers will vary. Sample response: *Humans have harmed black-footed ferrets. In the early 1900s, ranchers killed millions of prairie dogs. Ferrets could not survive without prairie dogs. Humans have also helped the ferrets. When scientists discovered a group of ferrets in the 1980s, they took them to a center. They helped them breed, gave them medicine, and taught them survival skills.*

page 61
1. a **2.** b **3.** b **4.** c **5.** c **6.** d **7.** c **8.** a
9. Answers will vary. Sample response: *Humans have harmed black-footed ferrets by killing millions of prairie dogs in the early 1900s. Ferrets could not survive without prairie dogs. Humans have also helped the ferrets by helping them breed, giving them medicine, and teaching them survival skills.*

page 64
1. c **2.** c **3.** d **4.** c **5.** a **6.** b **7.** b **8.** d
9. Answers will vary. Sample response: *Humans have harmed black-footed ferrets by killing millions of prairie dogs in the early 1900s. Ferrets could not survive without prairie dogs. Humans have also helped the ferrets by helping them breed, giving them medicine, and teaching them survival skills.*

CONNECTING THE WORLD

page 68
1. d **2.** c **3.** a **4.** d **5.** a **6.** c **7.** c **8.** b **9.** d
10. Answers will vary. Sample response: *Google probably wants to bring the internet to people around the world because getting online can change people's lives. Farmers can learn about new crops and order seeds. Doctors can read about new ways to treat people. Villagers can find new jobs.*

page 72
1. c **2.** a **3.** b **4.** a **5.** b **6.** a **7.** c **8.** d **9.** a
10. Answers will vary. Sample response: *Google probably wants to bring the internet to people around the world because getting online can change people's lives. Farmers can learn about new crops and order seeds. Doctors can read about new ways to treat people. Villagers can find new jobs.*

page 76
1. b **2.** b **3.** d **4.** c **5.** d **6.** b **7.** c **8.** a
9. b **10.** Answers will vary. Sample response: *Google probably wants to bring the internet to people around the world because getting online can change people's lives. Farmers can learn about new crops and order seeds. Doctors can read about new ways to treat people. Villagers can find new jobs.*